TOODY BYRD TALKS
AND TALKS
AND TALKS
AND TALKS
AND TALKS
AND TALKS...

BY

TOODY BYRD

Illustrated by Mark Hurst,
With special contribution by granddaughter, Ashley
Woodson

Published by
T. Byrd Roadrunner Press
Austin, Texas

Toody Byrd
2007

To

Sissy

Without whom this book would still be
just a stack of video tapes covered with
dust and guilt, sitting forlornly in my bookcase.

Toody Byrd Talks About...

ACKNOWLEDGEMENTS

I am indebted to so many people for the part they have played in my life and in getting this book written, if I were to list them separately that would be a book within itself. But there are a few I do want to thank for their help and encouragement through this endeavor and many others.

TO MY FAMILY:

***Hoyt Byrd** for hanging in there with me through good times and bad and in sickness and in health, just as he promised to do fifty-four years ago when we married.*

*My children, **Judy** and **Alan**, who let me "practice parent-ing" on them and proved beyond a shadow of a doubt that what works with one kid will not work with the other. One of my great-est joys is seeing them grow into caring, responsible adults who make good decisions, as evidenced by their choice of mates, **Ronnie** and **Kay**, whom I couldn't love more if they were my very own.*

*My wonderful grandchildren, **Jeffrey, Ashley, Hugh,** and **Kim**, who have by their individual uniqueness brought great enrichment, as well as a little spice into my life, kept me young, and showed me first hand what kids of today are thinking and doing..and for my newest grandchild, Jeffrey's wife, **Galeana** (a.k.a. Golly) who has brought joy and another funny name into our family.*

*My "Big Sister," **Pearle**, who has always believed I could do anything and convinced me of the same.*

***Larry** and **Cleve**, husband and son of my niece, **Sissy**, for tolerating the innumerable hours she sat at the computer tran-scribing from tapes to book.*

TO SIGNIFICANT OTHERS:

***MY STUDENTS**, each of whom has become a part of my life, and provided me with the "meat" for this book.*

MY TEACHER AND COUNSELING COLLEAGUES with whom I have shared both laughter and tears in our day to day journey to reach and teach/counsel our students. As we shared, we developed friendships which are my special treasures.

MOST OF THE ADMINISTRATORS for whom I have worked, for their leadership, friendship, inspiration, and cannon-fodder for my stories.

MEMBERS OF THE GUIDANCE COMMITTEE AT WESTLAKE HIGH SCHOOL for their support, hard work, and devotion, and to *THE WESTLAKE COMMUNITY* for making my twenty years in the school system such a rewarding experience.

JANN PHENIX-BROWN, CARL PICKHARDT, AND MARGUERITE DABBS for being the first people to talk about the possibility of turning my stories into a book and for their continued support, encouragement, and help.

MARY ANN RYMER, KATHY LUCKETT , AND TERRY HOLMBERG for their unfailing faith and loyalty.

CINDY MCWILLIAMS, whose wonderful photography made me look better than I really ever do, and *MARK HURST ,* who read my mind and drew pictures of what I was thinking.

Last, but far from least, NANETTE WIESE, Sissy's sister-in-law and the managing editor of a magazine in Washington, D.C., who read the book with an unbiased eye, gave suggestions for improvement, and edited it--all out of the goodness of her heart. Best of all, however, she said, "This is good. GO FOR IT!!!"

SO WE DID...TOODY BYRD TALKS...IS THE RESULT!

Published by
T. Byrd Roadrunner Press
Austin, Texas

Printing by
The Insite Group
Bryan, Texas

Toody Byrd Talks About Her Name and Credentials

YES, MY NAME IS TOODY BYRD!

Before starting this epistle, I think I will take care of a housekeeping chore--something that I know is bothering you a lot and you won't be able to sleep tonight if you don't find out the answer to it. Yes, my name really is Toody Byrd, and if I had another name I'd use it. I may be the only person in the world who likes to get an answering machine when I call somewhere for the first time. Otherwise I call and say, "May I speak to Mr. Johnson?"

The secretary says, "May I say who is calling?"

I say, "Toody Byrd."

There is this dead silence. Then she clears her throat and stammers, "I beg your pardon?"

I say, "Toody Byrd."

The next question is always, "Is that your real name?"

You know, like any fool would use a name like this and go through this routine every time you make a phone call if you had anything better to offer.

I asked my mother one time, "Mama, how could you name a little innocent baby Toody? It's just so funny."

She pulled herself up to her full five feet and

declared in no uncertain terms, "Honey, your name just got funny after you married that Byrd," adding, "Toody McDermett was a beautiful name."

Face it, Toody Byrd is a pretty funny name, so I usually start my speeches to groups talking about my name, but I had a different experience one time in Baton Rouge, Louisiana. There were about 500 teachers there, and I was milling around before my speech, meeting most of them. When I was introduced as Toody Byrd, nobody even raised an eyebrow. When I talked about my name at the beginning of my speech, nobody laughed very much. So when I got through I said to somebody standing around, "It was really strange; nobody even raised an eyebrow at my name."

"Honey," he replied, "if your superintendent's name was Poo Poo Thibodeaux, you'd think Toody Byrd was a pretty normal name, too."

But, when you have a name like Toody Byrd and a nasal West Texas twang that you speak with, you just learn to laugh first...and I think that's a pretty good thing to learn to do when you're working with kids...or teachers...or principals...or spouses. Because I've found it's a whole lot easier to laugh it off than it is to fight it out.

4

CREDENTIALS

In order to talk about working with kids you need to have worked with kids at every academic level. Well, I have worked with people at every academic level in my own home. I've lived with the Big Byrd for fifty-four years--fifty of those fifty-four years I've been telling him how to drive the car, and he has never yet done it to suit me. Obviously, he's a "slow learner!" And then, we have these two "a-little-above-average" children. You know, nobody really has average children -- all our children are a little above average. Our "little-above-average" children married two "little-above- average" children, and I'm happy to report they have blessed us with four "gifted and talented" grandchildren! I've always said if you want to know if a child is gifted and talented, ask his grandmother. My oldest grandchild sent me a dozen roses on my birthday when he was six weeks old; now, how much more gifted and talented can you be? So, I feel really qualified, having dealt with all these levels in my own home.

I also think you might be interested in some of my educational credentials. When you get to be my age and weight, about the only thing anyone is interested in is your credentials. I started teaching when I was eighteen and knew everything. I never have been that smart or that mean since. Not only was I a teacher at eighteen; I was the principal! I got to be the principal by default. I was teaching in this three-teacher school, and the teacher of the first and second grade was older than I, had more college, and should have been the principal. But she was newly married, and they lived right on the campus...and her husband didn't work...and she went home a lot during the day. So, she couldn't be the principal.

And then, we didn't have any kids in the third grade, but the man who taught fourth and fifth grade should have been the principal--everybody knows if you have a man in the building, he ought to be the principal. And he was one of the smartest men I've ever known, but he was eighty-nine years old and couldn't run fast enough to catch the big boys.   So that just left me, and why shouldn't I have been the principal?   I was eighteen...I knew everything...I'd had one year of college...and I could run like the wind! So, that's the way I started.

I have taught everything from all subjects in that seventh and eighth grade class to aeronautics in high school. I always taught required courses except the one semester I had a course called aeronautics in high school. We only offered it that one semester -- nobody elected to take it the next semester. As a teacher, I never had fewer than three preparations and usually had five, but I didn't gripe, and I didn't quibble, and I didn't know I couldn't do it. Besides, I thought the principal had learned what I had known from the very beginning: he was so fortunate to have somebody of my caliber on his staff--someone who could do any-thing. Well, I lived under this false illusion until I became a counselor and worked with the principal on a master schedule. The first thing he said was, "Let's give old Moody five preparations and maybe he'll quit." That did-n't do a lot for my ego.

I've also been the coach's wife. Now, in Texas, that is a rare opportunity. That's when you have to wait until after the ballgame to find out if you're married to the smartest man in the world or the dumbest SOB who ever lived (and it changed from week to week). I used to think there was nothing in the world worse than being the coach's wife until I became the quarterback's mother. Now, believe you me, that is worse. Alan Byrd quarter-backed from the time he was in the sixth grade until he graduated from Tyler Junior College, and I had chronic diarrhea the whole time. I missed every good play he ever made because I was in the bathroom.

Once Tyler was playing Ranger Junior College. Ranger is not too far from Cross Plains, my hometown, so we took my eighty-year-old Dad over to see his grandson play football. In the first half, Alan couldn't do anything right. He couldn't pass, and he couldn't hand off, and he couldn't run--he couldn't do anything. Some fool up in the stands kept on shouting, "Take ol' Byrd out! Take ol' Byrd out!" Well, I stood it about as long as I could and finally I stood up, turned around, and yelled,

"Will you just shut up!!"

...and he did.

The last half, Alan couldn't do anything wrong. Boy, he passed, and he handed off, and he ran, and he made two touchdowns himself, and we won the game. We got home and my Mother, who had waited up for us, asked, "Well, Daddy, how was the game?"

"Ah, it was good," he said, "It was real good. The last half, Alan just put on a real good show...and the first half, Toody did."

But you know, even when the kids were in junior high school, I couldn't enjoy the half-time activities because my daughter was the drum major. I had visions of that kid forgetting to toot that whistle and just marching everyone off into oblivion.

Well, anyway, I did all this stuff as the coach's wife and the quarterback's and drum major's mother while I was a teacher, and then I became a counselor. I became a counselor much as I became a principal: by default.

I was a perfectly happy, dynamic teacher of world geography to ninth-grade students at University Junior High in Austin when the avalanche--in the form of the principal, Joe Stepan--hit. It was the last day of the last week of the first semester when he came to my room during my "off" period and announced that both counselors had resigned (they *said* it was because their husbands had been transferred). He then, verbally, picked me up out of the classroom, put me in the counselor's office and said, "Now, learn how to be one."

I gasped, "What other choices do I have?" to which Joe replied,

"Well, you can go peacefully or we can fight it out, but either way you need to be in that office Monday morning." And on Monday morning, there I was.

After a number of years as counselor, I became the Director of Guidance and Student Services for Westlake High School and Eanes School District. Decoded, that is the Director of GASS. The superintendent gave me that title one time when I was off speaking and he thought I ought to be home working. He didn't even have the nerve to tell me himself. He came over and told my secretary. When I got back, she said, "Dr. Rogers said for me to tell you that he had made you the Director of Guidance and Student Services, and then he just sat down and laughed and beat his leg and said, 'You tell her I made her the **Official** Director of GASS.'"

Filled instantly with the "get even" venom, I said, "I'll fix him." Since this was before E-mail, I got out this school memo pad and wrote:

> *Dear Dr. Rogers,*
> *Mrs. Rymer tells me that you have*
> *made me the Official Director of GASS.*
> *Does this mean that when I became a big*
> *enough "pain in the ass," you made me the*
> *Director of GASS?*
>
> > *Love & kisses,*
> > *Toody Byrd*

Mary Ann, my protective, professional secretary, started to type, stopped and began to beg, "Please don't send it... please don't send it..." to which I assured her,

"I'm going to send it, and I'm going to send it in the in-school mail, too."

The next morning, Mary Ann came in. She didn't

even buzz me. She just walked in with her eyes big as saucers and said, " O.K., Miss Smarty, Dr. Rogers is on the phone."

I picked up the telephone and said, "Hello" in a sweet, innocent, slurpy voice.

"Yes," he said...and hung up.

I thought you'd like to know about my credentials and status in the community.

Toody Byrd Talks and Talks and Talks and Talks and Talks...

Toody Byrd Talks About Parenting

WE LOVES 'EM 'CAUSE THEY BELONGS TO US!

I got the idea for this parenting title from my son. One day, when he was about three, he had really been a devil all day long. I got him out of the bathtub, and I was drying him off. I just hugged him up to me because he was so nice and clean and smelled good...and I was going to be putting him to bed and not have to deal with him for eight hours. Hugging him, I said, "You know, Alan, you are such a stinker, I don't know why I love you."

He backed off and, with the certainty common only to 3-year-olds, said, "Lady, you loves me 'cause I belongs to you!" Which was the perfect answer, and I tried to remember that even when they weren't very lovable. That we loves 'em 'cause they belongs to us.

I've worked most of my life with kids in the middle school years on up, so I really didn't think much about talking to parents who had younger kids until it finally occurred to me: *this* is where it is. That if you, as parents, don't talk to kids when they are little about why the grass is green or why helicopters don't hit God, chances are they're not going to talk to you about premarital sex when they get to high school.

14

I remembered that I'm not much of a gardener. I'd just throw out these seeds every year, and I'd keep asking my husband, Hoyt, "Do I have any blooms yet...do I have any blooms...are they blooming?"

Finally, he said, "Hell, Toody, you don't want to weed 'em and water 'em...you just want to watch 'em bloom!" And I thought, this is the way it is with kids. In high school, we want to watch them bloom; but if we, as parents and teachers, haven't weeded them and watered them when they're little, they're not going to bloom in high school.

There has been so much emphasis on academic excellence, and how much pressure we have to put on kids to be sure they'll do as well as the Japanese, and how many new programs we're going to have to have to get them "up there." I'm worried that we may become "program-wise and people-foolish." We need to teach our kids that learning is fun. That it's o.k. to be curious until you die. Ask them when they come in from school, "What did you learn?" not "What grade did you make?" *We always ask them what they made--even in kindergarten-- and then we wonder why they are so grade conscious.* I want us to be real careful about the pressure we put on kids.

15

I agree with the person who first came up with the idea that childhood ought to be a journey and not a race. Don't let your kids grow up too fast. If you can, teach them that there are fun things to do at every age, and if they grow up too fast, they miss them. I remember saying to my daughter, "No, Judy, you cannot wear lipstick when you're in the third grade. If you wear it in the third grade, it's not going to be fun when you get to high school."

My daughter called me one day when her own daughter was little and said, "Mama, I'm so mad at you I could die! The one thing I hated the most for you to say to me when I was growing up was, 'No, Judy, you can't do that -- there are fun things to do at every age.'" She continued, "I just got through hearing myself say to Ashley, ' No, Ashley, you cannot have a bra when you are 3 years old. Bras are fun things to have when you've got boobs to put in them. If you do it now, it won't be fun later.'" Judy added, " It makes me sick at my stomach to hear your words pouring out of my mouth."

So, don't let your kids grow up too fast -- don't let them get on that fast track.

I'm always hearing mothers talk about how tired they are because they are having to take their kids from here to there. Well, you are not going to get any sympathy from me. I have yet to see a little 4-year-old girl screaming and crying to take ballet lessons. And I have yet to see a little 5-year-old boy who wouldn't rather play with his dog than put on that hot uniform and go try to hit that ball with that bat and miss it every time. These are things *we* want them to do! I used to ask my daughter when I would call her during the summer, "What kind of uniforms do the kids have on today?" (I thought that comment was a whole lot funnier than she did.)

Another thing to remember about parenting as your kids get older is, "Don't invite dependence." Let those kids move on. We try to keep them from making all the mistakes that helped us grow up. I can remember telling my daughter, "Judy, I know you're going to make some mistakes, but there must be ten million mistakes out there. Why have you chosen the same ones that I chose?"

But they've got to grow. If they can make mistakes and live with the consequences at home, where they have some support, it's a lot better than if you protect them from making any mistakes. They are going to make them sooner or later! It always bothers me when a senior's mom says to me, "This child has never caused me a minute's trouble." It bothers me a lot...because I am just hoping that when this kid gets away from home she has someone equally as nice to "follow" as her mother, because she hasn't made any decisions of her own.

On the other end of the spectrum, a lot of people who consider themselves "good parents" think they are the ones who give their kids lots of running room, lots of "unconditional love." And they think unconditional love is not giving them any direction. Unconditional love is not a non-directional form of parenting. It's where you set boundaries and hold to them. And you love them enough to let them suffer the consequences. I think the thing parents and teachers need to remember about kids is that we are the knot at the end of the rope. Stephan Glenn, the psychologist, says parents should give their kids enough rope to burn their hands, but not to hang themselves. I agree.

We can get really tired of dealing with all these things with our kids, but still--the time to do it is when they are still living at home with their folks who "loves em 'cause they belongs to us."

TEACH YOUR KIDS TO BE CURIOUS

I was going to school one morning, and I passed this little boy with his head real close to the ground. I watched him for a long time, and he didn't move. Finally I couldn't stand it anymore--I stopped the car, got out, went over to him, and asked, "What you doing?"

He looked up and said matter-of-factly, "I'm looking in a hole."

"What do you see?" I asked.

Here was a kindergarten kid who had already learned to pass the buck. He looked at me and challenged, "You look and tell me what you see."

Deciding I was up for the challenge, I got down on my hands and knees and looked in the hole. He again asked, "What do you see?"

"Oh," I said, "I see a legion of Roman soldiers marching. Now they are getting into their chariots."

He pushed me aside and said, "Let me see!" He put his eye to the hole, stayed a full minute, then looked back at me.

"What do you see?" I asked him.

Talk about a generation gap--he raised an eyebrow, gave me a disgusted look and replied, "I don't see all that junk you do."

I countered with,"Well, what <u>do</u> you see?"

Without a moment's hesitation, he informed me, "I see a bunch of robots, and they are just flying everywhere,

and there is a man on Mars."

I pushed him aside and said, "Let me see."

Well, we "let me see'd" back and forth until I realized we both were going to be late for school. So, I put him in the car and took him to the elementary school and walked him to the hall where the principal was standing.

"Billy, why are you late?" the principal asked.

Billy looked at him, flipped a thumb in my direction, and explained, "Me and her's been lookin' in a hole."

To the principal's everlasting credit, he looked at him and said, "What'd you see?"

Teach your kids that curiosity is just intelligence having a good time.

DON'T SWEAT THE LITTLE THINGS

Don't sweat the little things. If everything in your house is a no-no, nothing is. And kids don't learn how to differentiate between, "Honey, I'd rather you didn't do that anymore" and, "I'm going to kill you, kid, if that happens again!" Save your big guns for your big wars.

I can remember going to my daughter's house one

time. Now, my daughter is an immaculate housekeeper. (Every other generation in our family has immaculate housekeepers.) You can eat off her kitchen floor (you can hardly eat off my kitchen table).   But she had these two little kids and this great big St. Bernard dog. She lived in Corpus Christi where it rained a lot. On this visit, the back door opened, and in came these two kids and this big ol' dog--and they were all just as muddy as they could be.

Judy went all to pieces. She threw the biggest fit I have ever seen. I just went to the back of the house. She whipped the dog, took him outside, and bathed him; then she bathed the kids and cleaned them up; finally, she mopped the kitchen floor and waxed it.   Then she came back to where I was and said, "Well, go ahead and say it."

"Honey," I cooed, "I wasn't going to say anything -- it's really none of my business."

"That's never kept your mouth shut before," she reminded me.

"Well, since you asked," I ventured, "I think that was probably the finest fit I have ever seen. If you had worked on it for fifteen years, I don't think it could have been more perfect. It was wonderful. **I'm just sorry you used it on mud**. What are you going to do when these kids come in stoned out of their minds? They've already seen the worst you have to offer."

Save your big guns for your big wars, or, as a sweet young thing from Georgia once told me, "Don't pole vault over peas."

TEACH YOUR KIDS TO FINISH WHAT THEY START

Whether you think they do or not, your children listen to what you say to them. I remember one time when our daughter was in the 2nd grade, her teacher, Mrs. Powell, called and said she wanted to talk to me about Judy's achievement test scores. She started laughing and said Judy's math test score was really low because she only did nine problems.

"Why didn't she do more than nine problems?" I asked.

"Well, I'll tell you what she told me," she replied.

The ninth problem was 9 x 7. Now, this was in 2nd grade--before the push for academic excellence. She got it right, but this was as far as she got on the test. She knew somehow that 2 x 9 was 18, so on the side of the paper, she had written 2 x 9 = 18 three times and then added a 9.

She had come up with the right answer--but it had taken all of her time.

Her teacher said she asked her, "Judy, why didn't you just look at that and know we hadn't had it and skip it?"

"Mrs. Powell," Judy said, **"my daddy says that just because something is hard, we don't just throw in the towel. We hang in there until we finish it."**

I was proud of her. It didn't do a great deal for the school's test scores. Of course, we then tried to teach her that there are times when there are things she wouldn't be able to do at her age, and she had to just move on.

IT TAKES TIME TO BE A PARENT!!

It takes a lot of time to be a parent. Can you remember how much time it takes to walk a city block with a 4-year-old boy? He stops at every crack in the side-walk to see if there might happen to be a cricket in it. He's curious--he wants to see everything--but, it takes forever. Finally, you pick him up and carry him. You're not up to it!

Take time to listen. Have you ever waited for a

3rd-grader to tell you about a movie? It will drive you up the wall. In the middle, she'll ask you, "What'd you think about that?" And what we've been thinking is something entirely different. But it's important to listen. Ask them what they've learned at school and then listen while they tell you. And don't think it's necessary at that time to correct everything they tell you that is wrong. Also, don't ask them if you don't have time to listen. I remember one time when I was a counselor, this kid came by my door and said, "Hi, Mrs. Byrd. How are you?"

I said, "Fine, how are you?" and then I turned and went into my office. He followed me in and said, "Mrs. Byrd, you want to know how I am? If you do, stand there and wait while I tell you. If you don't, don't ask. It doesn't matter to me if you don't ask me how I am, but when you ask me how I am, I think you want to know, so it's confusing for me when you turn and walk off." Take time to listen.

If you really want to hear what your kids are thinking, **drive the carpool**. I don't know what it is about kids and carpools, but they think--once the parents put their hands on the steering wheel--they become deaf. Kids talk about stuff that you couldn't pry out of them, so listen real carefully while you are driving that carpool. You may find out more than you ever really wanted to know.

Also, don't use it against them and don't tell them where you found out -- because that would be like killing the goose that laid the golden egg.   So, don't complain about driving the carpool--it can be a very enlightening experience.

Also, go ahead and put those old pictures that they paint up on the refrigerator. I know that before I die, Better Homes and Gardens is going to come out with a house that has all these pictures stuck on the refrigerator! I know it will be the "in thing" some time. And if your child comes in with a flower, take the time to put it in a vase.

Take time to share. Tell about when you were little. Tell them what your parents did, so even if their grandparents don't live around them, they still know they're a part of their world. My grandkids come over and say, "Tell us about when you said this to Mama...."

You better watch out about grandmothers! I can remember back in the dark ages when my daughter, Judy, was in high school and two-piece bathing suits were just coming out. She was bugging me every day for a two-piece bathing suit and I kept telling her "No, absolutely not."   She went to spend the weekend with my Mama and

Dad, and when she came home, she said, "Mama, I'm going to ask you one more time, can I have a two piece bathing suit?"

I repeated my "no" response, and she retaliated with,

"Well, Mammy gave me this picture and said for me to just show it to you."

Well, I had on a two-piece bathing suit--and not only that, I had rolled it up just as high as I could get it. She went on, "Mammy said, not to make a big deal, but to just keep showing this picture to you."

I uttered, through gritted teeth, "Well, Mammy can just buy you a two-piece bathing suit."

Judy's smug reply was, " Oh, she gave me the money for it."

So, be careful about grandmothers.

Take time to read to your kids. I think the most important single thing you can do is to read to your kids, even before you think they are big enough to know what's going on. Then, when they get bigger, let them read to you -- and that will be pure agony sometimes.

I can remember when my son, Alan, read <u>Chippy Chipmunk's Vacation</u>--and Alan is now forty-seven. I remember it like it was yesterday. He didn't miss any words, but he didn't read it in a very smooth manner. I punished his sister by threatening, "If you don't behave yourself, I'm going to make you listen to Alan read Chippy Chipmunk's Vacation."

Read to kids in groups. I had a group of kids one time who were all delinquents. They had either been to reform school or were getting ready to be sent. I had them one period a day.

When I told them, "We can do whatever you want to do for one day a week. Tell me what you want to do."

"Read to us," they said. They were 9th graders.

"But you have to read what we want you to," they stipulated.

We started with True Confessions, but pretty soon they asked me to read out of their English books. They had never been read to before. They didn't move a muscle. One of them moved his chair up right by my desk...while I read, he would twist my hair, which was long at the time (I now have a bald spot). But they did so much better in their classes because they had learned to listen. And every once in a while, one would say to me, "I've got a little thing I'd like to read to the group." I think you can't give your kids a better gift than reading to them.

It takes time to be a parent.

HOLD ME TIGHT!!

All of our kids--and we did the same thing, although we may not have known names for it--go through the same stages. The first one is "hold me tight"--and that is what you have to do with babies, because if you don't, they'll literally flop out on the floor. We're really comfortable with that stage. We may get tired of them sometimes and think if somebody doesn't take this crying kid, I'm going to scream---but we are really necessary; we like it, because they can't do anything without us. We are really important to them; so, we can hold them tight and feel good about it.

But can you remember when your kids were little that it wasn't very long before they were past this "hold me tight" stage and were twisting and squirming? They had reached the "put me down" stage, and we were pretty comfortable with that. We knew that if we didn't put them down, they wouldn't learn to crawl and walk, so this was also a necessary stage. But still, we were really important to them. They couldn't do anything without us-- we fed them, bathed them, changed their diapers--so "put me down" was another comfortable stage for us.

Then they reached the "turn me loose" stage. When kids first get into this stage, they want to put their clothes

29

on by themselves and always have extra buttonholes left over. Or they come out with these ungodly combinations. We're not quite so comfortable with this development, 'cause they look real tacky, and we want to straighten them up and button that button where it's supposed to go. And we want to choose their clothes, so we won't want to throw up when we look at them. But still, that's a way of growing, too. This is where they jerk loose from us and run out into the street and scare us to death. But, they are trying their wings a little bit. This is where they say, "Let me do it; I want to do it myself; let me," but "you be there when it's time to eat." And, at that age, they still like you pretty well and don't mind going to the movies with you or to Grandma's for Thanksgiving or Christmas. Well, enjoy it--'cause they're going to reach this other stage pretty soon which is....

Let me go! And we are *not* comfortable with this, because we aren't sure if they fall down, they'll want us to pick them up. We're not at all sure that if they go out and can't get home, they'll call us to come get them. So, this is where this adolescent stage becomes such a big deal-- because we are not as necessary as we used to be. (And I think whether we'll admit it or not, we like to be needed.)

TURN ME LOOSE!

These kids have been so nice up to this point, and they

have lulled us into thinking it's always going to be that way--forget that!   But they are trying to spread their wings. You know, a cocoon is a warm, safe place, but the butterfly can't fly until he gets out of it.   And while we've let them crawl, because we know it is necessary for walking, and we've let them even wear those tacky things, when they get to adolescence, we are real worried about them. We wonder, "Have I taught them enough? I can't be with them every minute. What am I going to do?" This is a real important stage for both them...and us.

If you think some things you see when they're teenagers that you've seen before, you really have. They are similar to 2-year-olds.   It's this, "No,"and "I can do it." I sometimes think the main difference between 2-year-olds and teenagers is that teenagers are potty trained. They're still trying to step out on their own. As soon as they get into the teenage stage and get this boy-girl thing going, however, they revert back and it's "hold me tight." They even use the same language that we did with them -- it's "sweetheart" and "baby" and "darling." I went by my grandson's closed door at Christmas one year when he was a sophomore at USC and I listened to the sounds coming out of his room, and from the language I heard, I hoped he had a baby in there!   I don't think he did.

This "hold me tight" is what happens all over again. But I deal with a lot of teenagers who have been going steady, and suddenly, one or the other of them has reached the "put me down" stage. They don't want to be held so tight. Now, one wants to be held tight, and the other wants to be put down. You see these things evolve again and again.

Of course, then our kids grow up, and we go back to the taking care stages with our parents. Sometimes we're caught in the middle between aging parents and little kids or adolescents. We're often sandwiched in between both ends of the totem pole while we are trying to raise our kids. This is not an easy time.

MOTHERHOOD

I am not a shining example of a great homemaker. As I have said before, every other generation of mothers in our family is. My mother was. My daughter is a wonderful homemaker and interior decorator. I went for Christmas a couple of years ago, and her house was absolutely beautiful. One of her friends came up to me and said, "Oh, Mrs. Byrd, does Judy get her talent from you?"

My immediate reply was, "Lord, no, my house is early tacky."

I'm not a nutritionist, either. My breakfast every morning consists of a big ol' coke and a Hershey bar. Being a terrible cook, too, the height of my ambition is to eat out every night. When I was teaching, just before school was out each afternoon, I used to get out this mirror and practice looking tired. If I could look tired enough when I got home, the "Big Byrd" would say, "Oh, honey, you look tired, do you want to eat out?" Oh, yeah! yeah!

I also do not sew. I thought I would sew because my Mama did, so for the first twenty years of our marriage, I bought all this material. I'd buy these patterns, and I'd lay them out on the cloth and cut around them, and then I'd put the cut-up material in this big box--but I never did sew up a thing. As long as I didn't, I could convince myself that when I sewed it up, it would look just like Mama had made it. It wouldn't have; it would have looked just like I had made it. So I never sewed, and the box just kept getting bigger and bigger and fuller and fuller -- and I didn't feel like I was a very good mother. Finally, one day I was teaching--I really was a good teacher--and I was giving this dynamic demonstration. Right in the middle I thought, "There is not a way in the world my Mama could do this--so I don't *have* to sew."

I guess this is one of the things we all have to come to grips with. We have to be comfortable with who we are, regardless of who that is, because we can't be comfortable with anybody else if we're still trying to find out who we are. I used to tell the kids I worked with, "Half of being smart is knowing what you're dumb at." Play to your strengths. You can be a good mother, even if you are not exactly the kind of mother your mother was. I learned so much from my mother just by watching her, but I didn't learn any homemaking skills because she was always so efficient, she'd say, "I'd rather have your room than your help." But she taught Judy to cook and sew--she had lots of time with the grandchildren.

What I've learned about parenting, I've learned from a lot of places. I learned a lot from my mother. My mother did not take things lightly. If I wanted to do something, I would ask my Dad first, because he was often a real pushover. If he didn't want me to do it, he'd say, "Go ask your Mama."

I'd ask Mama and she'd say, "I'll think about it." Well, I knew I wasn't going to get to go, but she wouldn't say no, she'd always temper it with, "I'm going to think about that, honey, 'cause I love you so much I want you to do everything, but I want

to make sure that I love you wisely and not just too well."
I've tried to remember that.

I've also learned a lot from my mother-in-law. I
was married five years before I knew everyone in the
world didn't love me--then I got to know her better. But
one thing she did for me was make me a wonderful mother-in-law. I know everything not to do. My children's
spouses like me a lot better than my kids do, so I've
learned a lot about being a mother-in-law.

I've also learned a lot from my own children. And
let me tell you, if you have young children, don't believe
that what worked for the first one is going to work for the
second one. Judy Byrd was our first child. I hardly ever
spanked my children--not for their benefit, but because it
almost made me physically ill. So we did a lot of talking.
Judy is today--and was when she was three years old--the
most organized, methodical person in the world. You
couldn't **make** her do anything, but you could usually talk
her into doing most things--if you had the time. But one
day when she was three, I had just run out of time, and I
spatted her on the seat and walked away. She threw herself on the floor and screamed bloody murder so you
could hear it a city block. I just went to my room and
threw myself across the bed. She screamed and wailed

and would listen to hear if I were coming, and then she screamed and moaned again. Finally, she came to where I was and said, "Now, Mama, look what you've done. My face is all red. And you made my little eyes swell up. Why did you spat me? Why didn't you just talk to me? I'm a reasonable child." She is still a reasonable child and is the only person in my life who can get me to do anything in the world, because everything she says is reasonable and logical. She just out-thinks me on every point. If you really wanted Judy to do something, you'd say, "Now, Judy, I don't think you could do that in a hundred years." She would clamp her teeth together and give me a look which left no doubt of her message: hide and watch.

My son used an entirely different philosophy. If you said to him, "I don't think you can do that," he'd say, "You're probably right, so I'm not going to waste my time on it."

Alan didn't know he could talk until Judy started to school two years before he did, because she'd say, "Shut up, Alan, I'll tell it."

I was so organized I would go to the grocery store every morning. It was before the time of seat belts, and Alan would stand up in the back floorboard and lean over and talk to me. Every morning he would want to buy a

Little Golden Book at the store. One morning he said,
"Today, I'm going to get a *Little Golden Book*, and I want
to get the one about the frog."

"Now, honey," I said in my reasonable-mother voice,
"*Little Golden Books* cost too much money, and you can't
have one every day. And you cannot have one today."

He didn't ask for any long explanation. He just
crawled over the seat and put his arms around my neck
and kissed me on the ear and said, "Mama, I was just
telling the boys I played with yesterday that I bet I had the
youngest, cutest mother in Sweetwater."

Well, I just pulled that old car over to the curb and
gathered him up in my arms and said, "Sweetheart, we're
going to get you two Little Golden Books today."
(Because I didn't want him to think that kind of stuff does-
n't work.)

I am a wife, a mother, and a grandmother--and
believe me, the easiest and maybe the best of the jobs is
that of grandmother. One of the most fun things about
being a grandmother is you see that this kind of soft soap
treatment is hereditary. Alan has a little girl who manages
him just like he did me. He called me one day and asked
me if I wanted to hear the episode about the dogs, and I
said I did. It seems he had gone to buy a puppy and had

taken Hugh(who is the older of the two kids) and Kim with him. They went to this pen where there were ten puppies, and Kim went over to this little dog, picked it up, put it under her arm, and said, "Now, which one is Hugh's?"

#1 Son replied, "Kim, we are just going to get one dog."

"You aren't going to get Hugh a dog?" she asked.

I said, "No, we are just going to get one dog."

Well, she walked over to the owner of the dogs and asked in a voice filled with disgust, "Can you believe that this man is not going to buy my brother a dog? Hugh needs a dog."

"So, what happened?" I asked.

"Well," he said, " I grew up with this mother who said 'don't sweat the little things,' so I've got two dogs and two happy kids--and a wife who won't speak to me."

He called a week later and asked, "Do you want a second chapter to the dog story?" I said I did. "Kim came in a while ago and said she was going outside to play with the dogs. I told her she couldn't go outside to play with the dogs until she cleaned her room."

Kim put her hands on her hips and said, "*I said* I'm going outside to play with the dogs."

Since he had lived with this woman (me) who said if you are going to speak with little children you must get down on their level, he said he got down on his knees and looked her right in the eye, put his hands on her shoulders and said, "Kim, let's get something straight. You cannot go outside to play with the dogs until you clean your room."

He then told me, "That little thing put a hand on each of my cheeks and kissed me right on the nose and said, 'O.K., Handsome!'" I asked him what he did and he said, "Well, *we've* been outside playing with the dogs, and now *we're* inside cleaning up our room."

These are just some of the things I learned at home with my family.

OREO COOKIES

For you working mothers out there who are trying to do your job while you're also trying to be perfect wives, mothers, lovers, and "cheap" cooks and bottle-washers... forget it! It's not possible. Don't try to be all things to all people. You just can't do it. I worked two years, and then I had my little Byrds. I didn't work anymore until they

40

started to school...but I didn't want them to know I'd gone back to work. After I started to work full-time, I tried to do everything for them that I'd done when I was home all the time--and I nearly killed my fool self!

I am the world's worst cook. (My son said he was the only kid at A&M who didn't want to rush home to his mother's cooking.) I don't know when your kids tell you what they need for school the next day, but mine used to tell me just as I was putting them to bed.   I remember one night my daughter said, "Mama, I told my teacher you'd make fifteen dozen cookies for the Halloween Carnival."

"That'll be just fine, honey," I said. (This was begun with a "fakey" smile and finished with gritted teeth.) Then my son, Alan, added, " Well, Mama, I told my teacher you'd make twelve dozen."

"That'll be *just fine*, honey," I said. (same non-verbal communication). "When is the Halloween Carnival?"

"Tomorrow," they said in unison.

So, I put them to bed. Their daddy was already in bed, and I'm up at midnight stirring up those cookies, putting them on a cookie sheet, putting them in the oven...burning them, throwing 'em out and starting over. Finally, about 2 o'clock in the morning, it occurred to me that little kids like Oreos. You know, it's only the teachers and the room mothers who care whether those cookies are home-baked. So, I bought all these Oreos and put them on some of those disposable trays. I then covered the trays with foil---don't cover them with Saran Wrap.

That next night I took the cookies to the designated table in the library--I watched until nobody was looking. I then eased into the room, quickly put my cookies on the table, and eased out. Then I came back in, and in a little bit, one of the room mothers walked up to the front of the room. She raised the foil, looked horrified, and put it back down. The teacher noticed, walked over to her, and whispered, "What is it?" The room mother raised the foil to show her.

The teacher threw her head back, and with the back of her hand on her forehead, mouthed, "Oh, my God!"

By this time, the other room mother, who was way in the back of the room, asked in a loud voice, "What's the matter?"

The teacher clasped her hands together, froze everyone in the room with an "evil eye" and exclaimed in a voice filled with a combination of horror and disgust, "*Somebody* has brought *bought* cookies."

I rose from my perch in the back of the room, struck

my forehead with the palm of my hand, and said, *"God forbid!!!"* It just made my day.

So if you're trying to do all things for all people, just forget it. Believe me...trust me... <u>the kids always ate the Oreos first!</u>

THE VOODOO OF WORRY

We all--especially mothers--think we are not good parents unless we worry a lot.

I have this wonderful psychologist friend who always says, "Mothers have this firm belief in the 'Voodoo of Worry.' They are sure that if they stay up and walk the floor in the living room that their daughter will not get pregnant in the back seat of a car."

My mother-in-law didn't like me much anyway, but she really didn't like the way I parented, because when my kids were in high school and would leave to go on a date, I would go in to bed at bedtime and go to sleep. She thought that was awful and told me, "I always walked the floor until Hoyt got in." (I thought to myself, remembering our youth, that might not have been a bad idea.) She went on to ask, "What are you going to do if they have a wreck, and you get a call from the hospital?"

"I'm going to go down there," I said, "and I'm going to be real glad I had three or four hours of sleep before I got there." So, don't invite trouble.

Also, remember that stress is contagious. I like to go to the elementary school and watch parents drop their kids off. You can see them eating their kids out before they get out of the car; then the kid gets out and drops his books, and they go at it again; and then--just before the kids leave--they smile and say, "Have a nice day." The kid staggers away like some kind of zombie. Remember-- stress is contagious and worry counterproductive.

YOU EXPECT MORE FROM YOUR KIDS - AND THEY EXPECT MORE FROM YOU

You need to remember that you expect a whole lot more from your own kids than you do from other kids. My kids used to say I would come home from school and tell them, "Well, Jim just made 35 on his spelling test today, but he didn't feel very well. He'll do better tomor- row." The next day they'd ask what Jim made and I'd say, "Well, he just made 22, but he still had fever." Judy said she or Alan would come in with a 98 on a test, and I would say, "What did you miss?" I think we all do this. We let other kids have some leeway, but not our own--for after all, they are extensions of ourselves!

And while we expect more from our kids, let me tell you, they expect more from us than they do from anybody else's parents. I remember one time I had this high school kid tell me about seeing his friend's mother on Sixth Street, Austin's night spot.

" Mrs. Byrd," he raved, "she looked so cute. She had on this short, tight leather skirt, fishnet hose, and a little tank top. She was doing all the dances--she was the cutest thing"

"Golly," I said, "maybe your mother would like to go down there and do that."

He was quick to respond,"She'd better not!" They expect a lot more from you.

When my son was a senior in high school, there was this man--the father of one of the other kids--who had this flag, and he would run up and down the sidelines waving it every Friday night during the football games. I thought it was the yuckiest thing, and I found it necessary to talk about it every Saturday morning at breakfast.

My son always defended him, claiming, "I think it's the finest display of sportsmanship I've ever seen, and I think you ought to just shut up about it."

Well, I'd had that kid about up to "here," so one Friday morning, I said, "Alan, your daddy is going to run out with the flag at the game tonight." (Anybody who knows my husband would know just how funny this would be.)

"WHAT?" Alan gasped and then turned to his father, "You stay up in those bleachers where you belong! You are not going to embarrass me by running out there with that flag."

"Oh, honey," I cooed, " I thought you said that was the greatest display of sportsmanship you've ever seen in your life, and your Daddy is as good a sport as anybody."

Throwing his hands up in surrender, *Son* replied, "You have made your point, *Lady*, and, *Dad,* you stay in those stands where you belong."

So you need to remember this about kids: what's o.k. for other people's parents is not o-k for theirs, and the same is true for us as parents. What is o.k. for other kids to do is not o.k. for our kids. We need to be a little bit easier on each other.

BE REAL WITH YOUR KIDS

We run so many workshops now, and we write so many books on how to parent. We tell you exactly what to do about everything. You get to the point you begin to wonder if you'd know how to do anything if you hadn't read it in a book. You have good sense, and people have been raising kids forever. Regardless of what the books say when you're getting some help--**be sure it's you.**

This kid at school--whose mother had been reading books and getting ideas--came in to see me and said, "Mrs. Byrd, if my mother says to me one more time, 'That is your child speaking,' I may just kill her. Why doesn't she just say, 'Quit being a baby,' like she used to? I don't want to go into all that psychology stuff with her." So, whatever it is, be sure that it's you.

You don't even have to say anything sometimes for kids to know where you are coming from. A gesture and look can say a lot more than, "Hurry up before I scream!" Kids get the message. I remember one time my grandson, Jeffrey, was eating cereal at our house. With each bite, he spilled milk all the way to his mouth and back to the bowl. I had this cuptowel, and I was dabbing the milk up with each bite.

48

Stopping his spoon in mid-air, he raised a quizzical eyebrow at me and demanded,

"What's so bad about spilling a little milk?"

Somewhat taken aback, I answered, "Nothing, sweetheart, I didn't say anything about your spilling a little milk."

"No," he said, "but you sure had a mean face."

They learn a lot when we don't say anything.

PARENTS, GET YOURSELVES SOME BIG KIDS TO PLAY WITH

As parents, you certainly can't help your kids if you're bogged down in stuff of your own. Also, you ought to be comfortable as a couple, or even as a single parent if that's where you find yourself, because at best, these kids are just gifts we have for a little while. They are with us for maybe twenty years and then they are gone. If, as a couple, each of you has spent all your time and energy being just a parent, and are at odds with each other about what to do with the kids, when they leave at age eighteen, you're stuck with a stranger you may not even like. That is really sad.

Or, even if you are a single parent, and you have devoted your entire life to your child--without making any other friends or doing something on your own every once in a while--when that kid leaves, you are lost. I guess what I'm trying to say is, "Get you some big kids to play with!"

I think it's really sad when I hear a parent say, "I am my child's best friend." Believe me, kids like friends their own age. I have this one friend who said she was such a good friend to her kid she always encouraged her to tell her "everything." She says her daughter's in college now and she is still doing it--and the mother doesn't want to know.

I think it's important that you take some time to be a couple or a person in your own right. Another friend was divorced when her kids were in the second and third grade. She had enough money that she didn't have to work, so she just waited for her kids to come home every day. She put on her skates, the girls put on theirs, and they roller-skated up the street. If the girls wanted to play dolls, they all played dolls.

"I did that a whole year," she recalls, "I never did anything else or went out with anybody." Finally, one night her sister called inviting her for dinner because she had a new man she wanted her to meet.

"Oh, I couldn't do that," my friend cried, "I couldn't do that. I couldn't leave the girls."

The girls were motioning to her, "Go, go, go!"

She finally hung up, and asked, "What's with you girls?"

"Please go," they pleaded.

"But Honeys," she said, "I have loved being here with you. We've skated together and we've played dolls together...."

The girls looked at each other and finally the older one said, "We know, we know. We really wanted to skate with our friends, but we knew you didn't have anybody else to play with."

The same principle applies to older kids. I remember one of the saddest things I think I ever heard was when I was working with a kid with a drug problem in high school. " My dad wants to be my buddy," she said. "Mrs. Byrd, he's going to have to decide whether he wants to be my dad or whether he wants to be my pot-smoking buddy. Why doesn't he know that I have a lot of pot-smoking buddies, but I just have one dad?"

So, get yourself some big kids to play with, and then you can be a parent to your kids.

BE YOUR OWN PERSON -
THEN YOU CAN BE YOUR KID'S PARENT

In order to be a good parent, I think you first have to get comfortable with yourself as a person. You have to get comfortable with who you are and how you look --even if you're not very good looking. I believe we get stressed out when we think we are all created equal. You know, except in the sight of God, we are not created equal. Look around you. Some of us are tall and willowy, and some of you are short and fat! We try to be what we think we are expected to be.

When I give a speech, I always wonder how I'm going to look and what I'm going to wear; so, every year I buy a copy of Vogue magazine to see what the "new look" is. One year they will say, "This is the year of the tall, willowy look." The next year they will say, "This is the year of the slim, slinky look." I know that one year before I die they are going to say, "This is the year of the short, fat, red-necked matron look." That will be *my* year.

I can remember back ten years or so when if you didn't have Gloria Vanderbilt on the boob or Calvin Klein on your rear, you just weren't "in." I saw this white pique

dress in the store and it was on sale and it had Gloria Vanderbilt on the chest--I bought it! I went to St. Mary's University for a campus visit, and I thought I looked like hot stuff in my new Gloria Vanderbilt dress. Well, I couldn't find the admissions office, so I asked this kid on the campus. I could tell he thought I would never find it from his directions, so he told me, "I'll ride with you and show you."

He got in and I proudly straightened my new dress. He looked over and said, "You a nurse?"

Some of us got it and some of us ain't!!

Anyway, I have finally adjusted myself to the fact that if I keep drinking big ol' cokes and eating Hershey bars, I'm always going to be a short, fat, red-necked matron--and Paul Newman is never going to leave Joanne Woodward for me. That was the hardest thing for me to face, but I have finally accepted my figure, because it's easier than dieting or exercising. For me, exercise consists of waving from the car window.   My husband came in the other night when I was watching TV. There was this mountain of a man singing. "Hoyt," I said, "sit down; this guy is singing my song!"

He was singing, " I 'm made for comfort, I ain't made for speed."

IT'S A DIFFERENT WORLD - BUT KIDS STILL NEED SOME KIND OF STABILITY

When I was growing up, the world was really different from what it is today. The world was different when you were growing up from what your kids are dealing with today. When I grew up, I lived in the same house with the same parents on the same old ranch right outside of the same little town, where my Grandma and all my aunts and uncles lived. And that was a great deal of external stability. If my Mama wasn't home, I went over to Grandma's. If Grandma wasn't home, I went over to Aunt Ida's. That was an extended family that was there to give moral support. When my kids were growing up, we didn't live in the same house or the same town for all those years, but they lived with the same parents. We moved around, but we took our things. We moved as a family and put our things wherever we happened to be, so there was still some external stability.

Well, now it's not unusual for a senior in high school to have been in six high schools and to have lived with three sets of parents or guardians. So, the external stability often isn't there unless we work on it. But what these kids have learned to do--and I think it's real healthy--is to develop some internal stability. They are harder to deal with than we were. They ask more questions. They want to know why.

They question you when you come home. I think that's because we no longer are in a society where we have lots of time together. I can't tell you how much I learned when it was literally too wet to plow, and my Dad was home. But now, they have to stop you and ask--and sometimes it's after you've had a hell of a day anyway, and you just want them to leave you alone. But they've got to get these questions out. I don't think it's so much that they are as opposed to authority as it looks when they keep asking and questioning. It's that they just want to know-- they want to know if the thing you're telling them today is the same as it's going to be next week if they happen to be in Kalamazoo.

I have taught kids from the Panhandle to the Gulf Coast. I've taught kids who lived with ten people in a two-room shack and kids who drove to school in their own Mercedes. I've taught them when they lived with both their parents, next door to their Grandparents, across the street from Aunt Mary and Uncle John, and I've worked with them later when they lived with one parent, who has a different boyfriend/girlfriend every month.

And the kids we work with today have problems we never dreamed of -- AIDS, drugs, abuse of every describable kind and some that you can't even describe. When I speak at schools, I always tell the bus drivers that for many kids, they are the first adult the kids see in the morning and the last adult they see in the evening. And, you know what? I am so proud of these kids, because if I had some of the problems they have, I'd just pull the sheet up over my head in the morning and never get to school. But they come to school and they do remarkably well. However, I have to warn you, that sometimes what they are dealing with outside of school makes geometry a pretty low priority and sometimes even third-grade reading has to take a back seat.

We are all in this together, and we have to take time to meet our kids' needs and help them find some kind of stability.

THE THREE "I's"

As I've said before, kids today have problems we never dreamed of. You know-- drugs, gangs, AIDS, sex. I guess we dreamed about sex, but we didn't talk about it.

If we did, we didn't call it "sex;" we called it "it." We'd say such things as, "They did 'it'." You understand, it was always "they" and "them"...and never "we" and "us."

When I was talking to about 1,500 kids in Oklahoma a while back, I said, "Kids, I'm not nearly so worried that you will graduate from high school without learning the three "R's" as I am that you will graduate not knowing the three "I's": You are not INDESTRUCTIBLE. You are not IMMORTAL. And you are not INFERTILE!"

Kids used to come into my office where I had this chalk board, and I'd put a "zero" at one end of a long line and a "ten" at the other end. I'd say, "Kids, with zero being the least effective and ten being the most effective birth control, which is abstinence... trust me, HOPE is negative 10,000!" And that is what they use--a lot.

We need to face this and help them deal effectively with it.

KIDS ALL HAVE THE SAME BASIC NEEDS

Through the years, I have found out something about kids -- they all basically have the same needs. They have a need to be loved. They have a need to achieve something and get recognition for it. They have a great need to be accepted however they are. It doesn't matter where they come from or what they do, these are the basic needs that they all have.

There's another need I think kids have--a need to be useful. But I fear that too often the missing link is in the realm of service. The knowledge that there is fulfillment and satisfaction in making a contribution, however small, toward a job well done for humanity--even if it never gets their names on the front page, puts them in the upper income bracket, or rewards them with acceptance to Yale-- is invaluable.

Kids have a need to realize they are part of a whole world where everybody needs some help. I don't think kids who really get involved helping somebody else are ever quite the same. I think they become richer, regardless of what salary they may eventually earn. They need to learn what Edwin Markham wrote years ago, that "there's a destiny that makes us brothers; no one goes his way alone, and all that we send into the lives of others comes back into our own."

I was teaching migrant students in Corpus Christi back in the Dark Ages before we had "migrant classes." We just knew that we got them right after the first freeze in the Panhandle, and they left the first of April. We took up money for everything...these kids did not have a penny. They just barely got to school. They were not on welfare; their families just worked very hard, and their kids paid their way in one place before they went on to work for somebody else. We were collecting for the March of Dimes, and I went into my principal and said, "I'm not going to try to take up money for the March of Dimes from my kids. Just tell me how much you expect, and I'll save on my grocery money and put it in."

"Oh no you won't," he said, "You will ask these kids to contribute to the March of Dimes. You are going to learn something real important here. You won't get a dime from every kid in your class. But I'll tell you what you will get--you'll get something from every kid."

And I did.

You know kids were then just like they are now. They can find out anything that went on in the principal's office if they want to. The next day, Mary Ellen came to me and said, "Meez, why did you not want us to be able to do our part in the March of Dimes? Why did you want to deprive us of helping others who are not as fortunate as we are?" (I thought, Somebody has taught this kid a wonderful lesson. I hope I've taught my own kids the same.)

Mary Ellen kept standing, waiting for my answer. Finally, I said, "I wanted to do that, Mary Ellen, because I don't have a damn lick of sense." It was true. I was going to "save" them from their chance to realize that somebody was worse off than they were and needed their help.

Among their other needs, all kids still have that need to be useful, and we ought to reinforce it in them.

LEGACY OF NURTURANCE IS BEST DEFENSE AGAINST FUTURE "ME GENERATIONS"

A legacy is not something your children find out about after the funeral. It begins the day your first child is born and is based on the legacy your parents began the day you were born. A legacy is not just money. Money is the outward manifestation of a heartfelt belief that life and love are things to be shared with our children, with our friends, with the needy and with humanity, present and future.

Philanthropy is not something new to the 20th century. Evidence of it can be found in earliest recorded history. Egyptians and early Christians set aside something for the poor. Early American settlers built schools and churches, and later colleges and hospitals. All this was before they could get a tax write-off. Philanthropy then was based first on caring, then on sharing.

But things began changing in America, as things have a tendency to do. "Old money" evolved, and while people with names like Vanderbilt and DuPont amassed fortunes and left notable endowments, they bequeathed great trust funds not only for their children but also for the third and fourth generations. They assumed, of course, these future generations would continue to work, increase the fortune, and add to the endowments. In some families this happened, but in others it did not. I read of one family in Minnesota where this is the fourth generation in which no one has worked. Their fortune is gradually being used up, generation by generation.

I have a plaque in my office--and have given one to each of my children--which reads, "There are only two lasting bequests we can give our children....one is roots...the other is wings."

When we give our children roots based on too much money, we have made these roots so strong and binding that the kids can't pull away from them and use their wings. By taking away their need to work, we have deprived them of their knowledge of their personal worth and self-esteem. The wino on Sixth Street in Austin and the third-generation alcoholic on the French Riviera have one big thing in common: They are both nonproductive citizens. One just has enough money to look more socially acceptable and is probably having a lot more fun.

I would not have children (yours or mine) think I don't want them to have some money. I learned a long time ago that of all the labor-saving devices, money is the best one. But I feel about money just as I do about rope: I want them to have enough to burn their hands but not to hang themselves.

This may all be a part of the legacy my mother left me. I was really into "rights" when it had not yet become a popular concept. I was always saying to my mother, "I have a right" to do this or that. Her stock answer was always, "I'll tell you what right you have: the right to be useful. Everything else you have is a gift, and don't you ever forget it."

In cases where we have deprived our children of their right to be useful, they have assumed the right of entitlement, and we are mad at them about this. We label them selfish and call them the "me generation," when in reality we have set them up for this. We have not given them a legacy of caring and sharing.

I notice when I go by playgrounds, little kids are yelling, "It's my turn," and even as adults we want others to hurry and quit talking so we can have "our turn." Now it's our turn to decide what our legacy will be. And I hope when our children meet after the funeral and find out the last part of their legacy, they will listen, turn, hug each other and say, "Now it's my turn."

TOODY BYRD TALKS ABOUT STRESS MANAGEMENT

PUT YOUR OWN OXYGEN MASK ON FIRST!

We are always cycling through different things, and one of the big ones these days is "Stress Management." And I do think these are stressful times. We're moving so fast that we've got to have some real up-front ways to deal with things. My title for this is "Put your own oxygen mask on first." I got this from Sarah Weddington and from flying around different places. Before you ever get off the ground, they start backing the plane out, and the flight attendant comes on and, among other things, says, "I hope we have an uneventful trip. However, should the pressure within the plane lower, there will be an oxygen mask drop from the ceiling."

By this time, I am in a panic. I think I would not be aware of what to do regardless what she's saying, but she goes on: "Put the oxygen mask over your face...." But she also adds, "For those of you who are traveling with small children or other people you are responsible for, put your own oxygen mask on first, and then take care of others." I think that is where we are now. We need to "put our own oxygen mask on first"--to be sure that we take care of our-selves--so we are able to take care of others.

I had this friend who always used to say to me, "I

66

just want my life to level out, Toody, just to level out."
Well, one summer she worked as a volunteer at a hospital,
and she called me the first day and said, "Toody, they've
got me watching the heart monitors. I no longer want my
life to 'level out.' I just want to have the strength to cope
with the 'ups and downs.'"

I used to have this poster in my office with this old
cat whose hair was standing up on end, and it said, "Don't
talk to me about stress, tension is all that's holding me
together!" Somebody stole my sign, so I guess they needed it worse than I did.

We hear and read a lot now about things that stress
us out. But you know, the books are written and the support groups are there for the "biggies" in life: the big
things that stress us out--like death of a parent, or divorce,
or loss of a job, or death of a spouse. (You know, after the
third night in a row, I go to the bathroom in the dark and
fall in that water because my spouse didn't put the seat
down, I don't think the death of a spouse would be too
traumatic in my house.)

But I don't think it's the big things in life that stress
us out anyway. I think we can handle the biggies with
help. I don't think it is the mountain we climb that gets
us: I think it's that grain of sand in our shoe...these little,

itty-bitty, nitty-gritty things that happen to us day after day after day, that finally just stress us out. We need to learn to deal with these little things.

One thing that might help us is learning to do a little creative elimination. We just take on one job after another after another, but don't eliminate anything. After a while we are "up to here." For everything you add, take something away. It's kind of like your closet. If you haven't really "used" something in a couple of years, chances are you've outgrown it.

We've got to make our lives simpler.

WE'RE MASTERS OF THE "VAGUE WORD"

I think we get stressed out when people won't do what we want them to do, and sometimes they don't even know what that is. We are masters of the vague word--the word that means something to us and nothing to anybody else. My famous vague word at home is "considerate."

"You are just not considerate." "You used to be considerate." I can remember for one whole week one time, I put the Big Byrd's coffee down every morning luke warm, and I sloshed it in his saucer. (By the way, girls, if you want to make a point when you put their coffee down, put it in a cup and saucer instead of a mug, so you can slosh it.)   Then I put this burned toast down--he's used to burned toast, but I usually scrape it.

In my best long face and "poor-me" voice, I said, "You're just not considerate. You used to be considerate."

Well, the Big Byrd is the calmest man in the world, or he wouldn't have lived with me for all these years, but he can only take so much. Friday, I put his coffee down and sloshed it, followed by burned toast. He had this fork in his left hand, and he hit it on the table and said, "Dammit, Toody, what do you want me to do?"

"I want you to start my car in the morning, so it will be warm when I go out there," I whined. "You used to do that when you were considerate."

With a sign of utter disgust, he asked, "Why didn't you say that Monday?"

"It would have made my life too simple," I haughtily replied.

As I've mentioned before, I'm the world's worst cook--and the height of my ambition is to eat out every night. I can remember one day when I was teaching, I thought, "Oh, if I could just eat out tonight." I thought about it all day and the fantasy got bigger and bigger. I

thought, "I want to eat at Tres Amigos, and I want that chicken taco salad. I'm going to put guacamole and sour cream--both--on it. I don't care about the calories." I thought about it all day--but I didn't call Hoyt.

Well, he was sitting in his office and thinking, "Oh, if I could just get home tonight and get in that big easy chair, and get my shoes off, and get that TV puncher. I don't even care if I have to eat Wheaties again tonight, if I can just get home!" But, he didn't call me. We just dreamed these different dreams all day.

I walked in, and he had beaten me home. He was in that chair, had his shoes off, had that TV puncher, and was running up and down the channels like he always does. He looked up and smiled and said, "Hi, Honey! What's for dinner?"

I threw my hands in the air and roared in an upper level octave, "That's just the way you are!"

He said, "What'd I do???"

Let me tell you, if you want to do something in the evening, whether it's eat out or take your shoes off and stay at home--call in the morning. You may not get to do what you want to do, but you won't think you're going to get to all day!

Here is a misplaced footnote just for you fellows: If

you're going to take your wife or your girlfriend or some-
body else's wife out to eat and you ask her where she
would like to go and she says, "It doesn't make any dif-
ference" and you believe her, **YOU ARE DUMB!** *It may*
not make any difference, but if you don't go somewhere
she wants to go, she's going to pout all week.

NOBODY CONTROLS MY HAPPY BUT ME!

We also get stressed out when we think we don't
have any control. Well, just face it, you don't have any
control over anybody but yourself. You really don't have
much control over what happens to you, but you do have
control--if you take it--over how you allow it to affect you.
Haven't you seen two people who had almost the same
gory thing happen to them? One of them rolled around in
the misery of it for twenty years while the other one just
kind of thumbed her nose and went on. Nobody controls
my happy but me!

And if we want to talk about happy, let's talk about
the other end of it, which is mad. Can you remember the
last time you were really mad. When you finally got over
it, weren't you just exhausted? You know mad is the most
energy-consuming thing in the world. Well, if we're
going to spend that much time and energy on mad, I think
we ought to be real selective about who or what we let

make us mad. You know, most of the time we're mad at people we don't even like! And then, we don't have enough energy left to be nice to the people we do like.

When I was a counselor, I absolutely hated achievement testing, and I had this new principal at school whom I didn't like much better than I did the achievement testing. I had fought with that man all day long about achievement testing, and I walked in home that night, and the Big Byrd said, "Hey, Toody, do you want to go out and eat?"

Although, as stated before, the height of my ambition is to eat out every night, I said, "No, I'm too tired." Then I thought, "My God, what have I done to myself? I have used up all my energy on that man I don't like, fighting about something I like less than that, so that I don't have enough energy left to go out and do something I like better than anything in the world with this man that I love--no more!" I just have about five people in my life right now that I love enough to let them make me mad.

I think that sometimes when we're mad at someone we like, we think it's our Christian duty to spew this mad out on everybody else we see. I used to think I hadn't done a "good mad" at school if fifteen people didn't say, "You better stay away from Toody; she's mad at the world today." So let's try to keep this mad where it's supposed to be--even if we don't have enough nerve to do anything but pout about it.

Then, sometimes I think the only truly safe place to be mad is at home, because if you get mad and spout off on your job, you may not have a job. If you get mad and spout off with your friend, you may not have a friend. So the people we love the best may get our mads all the time. I used to live near a guy who had a wife and a little 3-year-old boy. Papa'd come in about three days a month just driving like a bat out of Hades and pull in the drive and have to throw on his brakes, because a tricycle was in the middle of the driveway. He'd jump out of the car, slam that car door, grab that tricycle, and throw it across the yard. He'd then open the front door (I've watched him fifty times; I didn't want to miss anything) and yell, "Billy, I must have told you ten thousand times not to leave that tricycle in that driveway; and Mabel, if you were any kind of a wife and mother, you wouldn't let him!"

I knew that Billy and Mabel were sitting chewing their nails, feeling miserable. But he wasn't mad at them; he was mad at something that happened at work. But he was in a safe place.

Maybe we have to do this, but if you're going to let

the people at home have the mad, warn them. Pull in like a bat out of Hades. Slam the car door. Throw the tricycle. Throw open the front door and say, "Now hear this: I am just madder'n the devil! Doesn't have anything to do with anybody in this house, but if you don't clear the runway, you're going to get it!"

We understand that. Little kids understand that. Now anybody who hangs around inside after that warning is asking for it.

VALENTINE'S DAY

I think we get stressed out when we come from a family of huggers and patters and gift-givers, and we marry into a family of hand-shakers, one-gift-a-year at Christmas, $10 limit.

I came from this huggy, patty, gift-giving family, and I married this Big Byrd, who came from the shake-the-hand variety! Now he gave me gifts before we married. I don't know when he lapsed back into his own family upbringing, but he soon just gave me this one gift--at Christmas.

Well, I thought I took it pretty well except at

Valentine's. Now Valentine's was/is a really big day for me. It's for sweethearts and lovers, and that's what he said we were, and that's what I believed. He never even sent me one valentine. Well, we'd been married for three years, and just before Valentine's Day that year I thought, "There is bound to be a way to lick this one!" So I went down to the drugstore, and I bought the biggest, laciest, gushiest, sweetest valentine that you ever saw in your life.

Well, the Big Byrd is left-handed, and he can hardly write where you can read it, so he always types everything. So, I took the card over to a friend's house, and I typed my name and address on the envelope. Then, I typed inside the card, "YOURS." Then I mailed it to myself.

On Valentine's Day, when he came home from work, I had this card in my hand, and I threw my arms around him, and I just hugged and kissed him and patted him and loved him, and I said, "Honey, I can't tell you what this valentine means to me! It is so wonderful that you finally realized how much this means. This is the prettiest, sweetest valentine! I just love you for giving it to me!"

Well, Hoyt Byrd is the most honest human who ever lived. I've often said that if he told me there was a purple cow in our yard, I wouldn't know how she got there, and I wouldn't know how in the world she got purple, but I wouldn't doubt him. Well, here is this honest man, and I am holding this card and hugging him and patting him and thanking him for the valentine he, obviously, hadn't sent. He finally backed up against the wall, smiled a sheepish smile and said, "I'm glad you like it."

Not until this day has he confessed he didn't send that valentine. But, you know, he still forgets our anniversary; he forgets my birthday; but he's never forgotten Valentine's Day again! I get candy and flowers--it's a big deal to him, too!

Remember - huggers and patters can also be creative.

DON'T GET BOGGED DOWN IN OTHER PEOPLES' PROBLEMS

I think we get real bogged down in problems that aren't even ours. My grandson used to come and stay with us--he did that from the time he was born. He slept in our regular size bed between his Granddad and me--I know Freud would flip over if he heard that, but we didn't think it was so bad. But no matter how I put that kid in the bed, the minute he went to sleep, he was perpendicular to us. And I'd hang off the side which is not the most comfortable way to sleep. So, I decided I'd buy him a sleeping bag. I didn't want this little bitty boy to get lost in a big old sleeping bag, so I spent a lot of time finding a little sleeping bag for him.

The next time he was staying with us, his Granddad had just finished bathing him and getting him ready for bed. I put the sleeping bag beside the bed, and when he came out he looked over at it, pointed a stubby finger and demanded, "What is that thing?"

"Honey, it's a sleeping bag," I said.

"What's it for?" he challenged.

"Well, it's for you to sleep in, Darlin'."

"I always sleep with you and Granddaddy Hoyt," he reminded me.

"I know you do, Sweetheart, but it's so crowded."

"I'm not crowded," he said. Then he went over and crawled up in his Granddad's lap and asked, "Granddaddy Hoyt, are you crowded?"

Well, Hoyt Byrd is just a pillar of strength to me, and he said, "No, Jeffrey, I'm not crowded."

So, Jeffrey turned to me and announced, "Well, Grandmother, if you're crowded, why don't you sleep in that sleeping bag?" Well, I had spent so much time getting that little sleeping bag, I wasn't going to waste it. I had to sleep with my knees bent--it was obviously my problem, but I had thought it was Jeffrey's.

You know mothers think their kids have a problem with dirty rooms. Kids don't have a problem with dirty rooms. Mothers do. Mothers also have the most opened-up sinuses in the world. They can smell a dirty sock a mile off. Kids' sinuses don't open up until they get married and have children of their own.

I had one mother come in and say, "All I want in the world is for that kid to have a clean room."

"If that's all you want," I told her, "do this...and this... and this, and I think you can get a clean room."

She came back in two weeks in tears, and said, "My son has not spoken to me in two weeks."

"Do you have a clean room?" I asked.

She admitted, "Yes."

"You didn't say you wanted him to speak to you," I said. "You said all you wanted in the world was a clean room. Maybe you're not going to get both of them. Maybe you are going to have to decide which you want. Or maybe, if you hold in there long enough you can outlast him--because he's going to have to ask you for money sooner or later."

You have to decide what is really important. Of course, what we really want is for someone to do what we want and be happy about it. But the room wasn't the kid's problem.

We really don't have control over anybody but ourselves. So we shouldn't borrow problems--we should just decide which battles we want to fight.

WHO'S AT RISK -- WE ALL ARE

Who's at risk? Certainly the kids are, but the teachers are too. At my school, we ran four divorce support groups for teachers, because it is really hard for any of us to be concerned about kids when we have huge problems of our very own looming over us. I was amazed at the teachers who came into my office for help when I was a school counselor and how well they did.

I had a parent ask me one time, "How do you justify spending a whole hour with a teacher when you were hired to work with children?"

"Listen," I said, "if I can get this teacher back together, I have helped 150 kids that day." So, I think teachers are at risk, and I think counselors should be trained to work with them. Because no matter how much good we do with a child one-on-one, that kid has to go back into that classroom with that teacher.

Who's at risk? Parents are also at risk. My last years of teaching were in a very affluent section of town at a time when the economic picture in Texas was really bad. One of my parents told me, "I want to tell you about fifteen families that are going to declare bankruptcy. And I want to tell you that out of that fifteen, ten of those fathers are going to disappear. I want you to know what to do to help the kids."

We are all at risk who try to help these kids--that is an energy-consuming kind of life. Sometimes I was so tired from having dealt with one calamity after another all day, that I would just think, "I've had it!"

So I needed something different when I went home. I went home one day and the Big Byrd said, "Hey, Toody, what can I do to make your life simpler and easier?"

"You can shut up," I said. "And don't turn on anything that talks. And don't make any movement if you can help it." He took one look at me and headed for the golf course.

We are all at risk. We have to learn to take care of ourselves.

KEEP AN ACE IN THE HOLE

One thing that I think will help you deal with stress is to keep an ace in the hole. Somebody who loves you best ...even if you have to make him/her up. You know, I used to tell these senior girls who'd come in crying because somebody had asked them if they had a date to the prom (you know who asks senior girls if they have a date to the prom--senior girls who *have* a date to the prom).

"Let's get you an imaginary boyfriend," I'd tell them. "Let's let him live in Houston or Dallas or El Paso. Let's let him have a common name like John Jones or Bob Smith. Don't let him live in Pflugerville, and don't let his name be Richard Mossesian. They can look for it in the phone book. They'll check up on you."

I told them to get this imaginary boyfriend, and the next time one of the smart-aleck girls asked them about the prom, to say, "Well, Bill and I are going steady, and he doesn't want me to go." Then, I said, "If somebody asks you to go - GO!" When you get there, if somebody asks, "What about Bill?" just say, "Oh, we broke up!" You cre-ated him--you can destroy him. That's what is known as an ace in the hole.

82

Everything that I wanted when I was growing up that we couldn't afford, my mother would say, "Don't worry about that, Honey. I'll get that for you when my ship comes in."

Well, I was a slow learner. I must have been fifteen years old before I realized that not only did that old woman not have a ship--she never had even seen the ocean.

I remember one time my son was giving me a hard time about something, and I just got up and went upstairs.

"Where are you going?" he asked.

"I'm going to go up and call Mike Looney in Denver, Colorado," I replied. Mike Looney was a student I had had fifteen years before.

"What for?"

I smugly informed him, "Because Mike Looney thinks I'm wonderful!"

I don't know if any of you remember old Chill Wills, an old cowboy star. But Chill Wills came to the Cross Plains Picnic when I was sixteen. He was, obviously, on the way down or he wouldn't have been at the Cross Plains Picnic. He gave me this 8 X 10 glossy print of him and he wrote on it, "To Toody, If you ever need anything, call me. Chill Wills." Well, I want you to know that I've moved that old glossy print from the Panhandle to the Coast five or six times. I've often thought, "Gosh, if things get any worse, I'm going to have to call old Chill Wills."

Before I retired from counseling, I was speaking in some "exotic" places. If they would give me a hard time at school, I would just go in my office and close the door and I'd say, "To hell with them; they just loved me in Poteau, Oklahoma!"

GET YOU AN ACE IN THE HOLE!

Toody Byrd Talks About Education

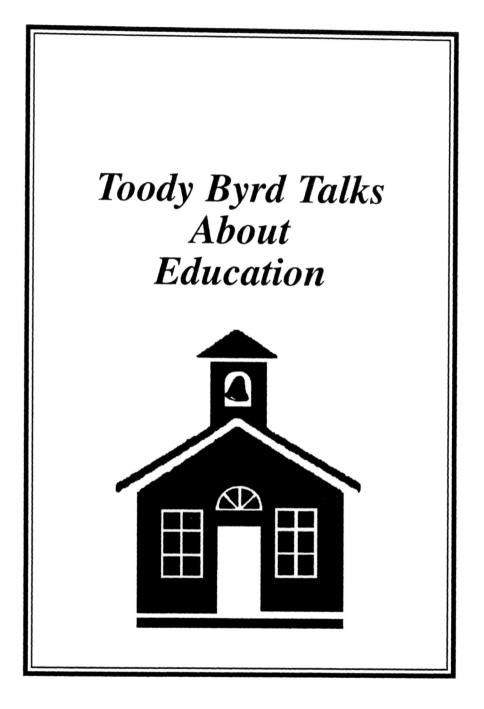

TO THE SUPERINTENDENT, SCHOOL BOARD, PRINCIPALS, AND TEACHERS --- REMEMBER ENTHUSIASM STARTS AT THE TOP

In all school systems, the superintendents really have the most important jobs in the district, but nobody thinks they do. Nobody in the community thinks they do--everybody thinks **they** know how to run the school. If you don't believe this, you can go down to the filling station and hang around and listen, or you can read the paper. The principals don't think they do because they don't have to do appraisals. The elementary teachers don't think they do because they don't have to get down on their knees to anybody and nobody throws up on them. The high school teachers don't think they do because they don't have to grade term papers, and coaches don't think they do because they don't have to put a team on the field every Friday night. The kids don't think they do because **they** don't even know who they are. And still....superintendents set the tone for the whole district. They've got to decide whether they are going to have exciting, innovative schools or whether their philosophies will be "Don't rock the boat, don't get out of line, status quo is good enough."

It is up to them because--contrary to popular belief, I think enthusiasm starts at the top.

How dare principals be enthusiastic if the superintendent is miserable? How dare teachers be enthusiastic if the principal is miserable? And I'm always having teachers say to me, "My eighth period class is so dull. Those kids are so bad. They are so spaced out." Do you know what I say?

"So are you, so are you," I tell them. "I go by your second period class and, man, you are up and at 'em! I go by your 8th period class and you've had it. How dare that kid be excited when you are burned out and tired? Save something back."

Superintendents have the hardest job, but we really need them. One of my past superintendents called all the new teachers in and said, "I want you to understand my status here. I was on my deathbed in the hospital this summer, and the Board voted 4 to 3 to send me a get well card."

But I want to also say something about the School Board members--they are the truly devoted educators. We, as teachers, talk a lot about long hours and low pay. Those people have long hours and no pay.

If you happen to be new in your job as a principal or

superintendent, let me give you two little hints: the first is "if it ain't broke, don't fix it," and the second one is to remember that "a gentle breeze will eventually blow away as much debris as a whirlwind, and that it won't stir up nearly as much dirt." And, if you happen to be a new teacher, let me warn you, "Don't make friends too quickly--hang around and see who the custodians like."

"FIX IT" THEORIES ON THE "WRONGS" IN OUR EDUCATION SYSTEM

Everybody knows there is something wrong with our education system today, and everybody knows how to fix it, but nobody agrees on the fix-it theories. They all come up with different theories: One is we need to use the business approach; another says technology will fix it; another one says we've got to get these kids earlier; someone else says it should be academics only; another one says we've got to keep church and state separate and prayer out of schools; another says values are important, but who is going to teach them? Everybody agrees that we've got to get those test scores up. While I think each of these theories has merit, I have concerns about each one, too.

As far as the business approach goes, I think we

ought to remember that businesses turn out products and schools turn out people. And the products that businesses turn out are only going to be as good as the people we turn out. We ought to remember that businesses have employees; we have kids. No matter how bad those kids screw up, we can't cut their wages and we can't fire them. We just get them back next year ... if we're lucky.

Technology bothers me because the word obsolete always pops up. They tell us to remind kids what they learn about technology as freshmen will be obsolete by the time they graduate. Maybe what technology is trying to teach us is that computers are just *tools* to help *people* function better, and we're going to have to be lifetime learners--flexible and mobile. And computers never claimed to take the place of smiles or hugs or pats on the back.

Then we say we've got to get these kids earlier. My Lord, we get them when they are four years old. At one year, they are nursing babies. At two years, they have a thumb and a blanket. Three years is not very long to be a little kid. Somehow, I've always thought childhood ought to be a journey, not a race.

The "academics only" theory is the one that scares me the most. I am convinced that if we educate their heads and not their hearts, we're going to turn out a bunch of intellectual barbarians.

We need not worry about prayer in schools too much, because as long as there are algebra tests, there will be prayer in the schools.

Every time we hear "values," somebody thinks we're going to talk about sex education. To me, values are when you tell kids it's not O.K. to be mean; it's not O.K. to lie; it's not O.K. to steal; it's not O.K. to destroy either property or people. I think those values ought to be taught at home, at school, at churches...wherever kids are.

We all agree we've got to get those test scores up, but not at the expense of everything else.

Maybe we ought to teach kids some things that are never going to be obsolete, like:

> It's always going to be as important that they have a chicken in every pot as it is that they have a computer on every desk.
> It's always going to be as important that babies are born with two parents who want and love them as it is that we have a five-year-old who can read the *Encylopedia Brittanica.*

That it's always going to be as important that kids learn that kids don't go around shooting kids as it is that they learn enough to score 1500 on the SAT. And there is now--always will be--dignity in honest work.

These things will never be obsolete.

CRISIS MANAGEMENT

You know, we did a lot of things in that old three-teacher school where I started my teaching career. We just didn't know what to call them. I remember one of the "joys" of being the principal was that I got to unlock the door every morning. It was an old building that had the water piped in after it was built. One morning in January, I unlocked the door, and the pipes had frozen and burst. Now, *that* was a *crisis*.

I grabbed this old school bell, ran upstairs, threw open the window, hung my head out the window, and started yelling, "Help! Help!" Now, *that's* called *crisis intervention.*

In ten minutes, all thirty-five people living in Cross Cut, Texas were down at the school. Now, *that's commu*

nity involvement. One of the guys looked up and said, "My God! We've got to cut up some inner tubes and wrap these pipes, and get this water stopped so she can get on with her real job. *That's real community involvement.*

So they came back and started wrapping the pipes. Since I was the principal, I told them how to do it. Now, *that's* called *on-site management.* The only thing wrong with on-site management is that you get input from other people whether you want it or not.

Finally, one of these guys said, "Toody, if you'll just shut your mouth and get out of the way, we can get these pipes wrapped and you can get back to your real job, which is working with kids."

Regardless of where we are or what new styles we have, that's our job as parents and teachers --- working with kids, because they are our hope for the future.

MY FEELINGS ABOUT THE COMPUTER

I know this will be blasphemy in this technological age, but when you get to be old and fat and retired, you can say anything, and I am going to tell you how I feel about the computer -- I just hate it. But I have finally come to grips with it. I have decided I feel about the computer the same way I feel about birth control pills. I think they are both marvelous new discoveries that have changed the ways of the world. And, for some people, I think they are absolutely essential--but at my age, I just don't need them.

I'm going to tell you some stories about my experiences with the computer. I was in the Eanes School District for twenty years, and about three years before I retired, we got this new business manager who put in this whole computer system. Now, I was used to dealing with the old business manager who talked in terms of people and money. This new one talked in decimal points. When he got this new computer system, he called us all into this staff meeting, and for two hours he explained the system to us. In five minutes, he reduced every person and everything that had a name to a number.

Martha Adams, who had taught freshman English there forever, was no longer Martha Adams. She was #11155.912356, and she was no longer teaching freshman English; she was teaching # 1900.1223456.

Then, two hours later, after talking all these numbers and decimal points to us, he said, "Now, if you have any problems with any of this, call my office and tell my secretary that you want to talk to me about 'Roger.'"

Jumping straight up, as if we had just lost the state playoff game by a three-point shot from the center line as the final buzzer sounded, I shouted, "The hell you say! You have reduced every teacher and everything with a name to a number, and you want me to call that damn machine Roger? You must be putting me on."

Well, everyone looked at me like I had lost my mind. I couldn't believe this, so I simply held my hands out, palms up, and asked, "Does this not seem strange to anyone else in this room?"

Then they looked at the ceiling or the floor or out the windows, but never at me--the silence lengthened until the superintendent, who knew me real well, spoke up.

"Bob, Toody just comes to these meetings every fifth time. Why did you choose this time to talk about the computer."

I never called about Roger. I had the only office on the campus without a computer, and the only button I learned to push on my secretary's computer was the one that always said, "Access Denied."

The Big Byrd is really into technology, and he bought me this car with this computer. It didn't talk to me; it just flashed messages. It'd say, "Left blinker on, left blinker on, left blinker on." I like having my left blinker on. It keeps the people behind me in doubt about what I'm going to do. It'd flash, "Twelve miles to empty, twelve miles to empty, twelve miles to empty." I just hated the thing. Not only did I know I was going to run out of gas; I knew I was going to have to walk three miles because the nearest gas station was fifteen miles down the road. And then the idiot thing wouldn't let you make a mistake. If I tried to lock my keys in the car, it'd just go wild. It would flash and blink and the horn would blow. It'd say, "Keys in the lock. Keys in the lock."

You know, the crazy thing didn't know how many interesting people I had met who had opened my car door with a coat hanger.

It wouldn't talk to me, but I got to where I would talk to it. I'd say, "I know the blinker's on; I know the blinker's on. Leave me alone!"

Friends who would pull up to the stop light beside me would ask, " Talking to the computer again?"

Finally, I just went to the Big Byrd and said, "I want you to get rid of that car. I am an interesting person. I do not have to go around talking to cars."

But computer people have a whole different vocabulary. They have all these acronyms -- ADC, ATR, VGA, VHS. It reminds me of this senior at Westlake who was walking out in the hall just before graduation, and I heard him say to his friend, "I've had the SAT, and the PSAT, and the ACT, and sometimes I think, Oh S-H-I-T, am I ever going to get O-U-T?"

But the computer language is a whole new language. I'm kind of like my friend, Kathy, who worked one summer as a receptionist in a computer office. This man called and said he needed to speak to Mr. Smith about the "chips and bites." Kathy called Mr. Smith and said, "Mr. Smith, Mr. Harazumi is on the phone, and he wants to talk to you about the refreshments." I don't know what a lot of these words mean, but some I can figure out because of my past experiences, such as:

BIT: This is a dash of something you put in cornbread. It would have been easier if they had called it a "little bitty bit."

CHARACTER GENERATOR: That's what you get when you lose a football game 43 to 0.

CHASING: It's what you do after you first get a divorce.

DESKTOP PRESENTATION: It's when a teacher leaves the classroom to go to the restroom, and when she comes back, there is an eighth grade kid up on the desk doing a tap dance.

DISPLAY SIZE: That's when you go in a dressing room to try on clothes, and you stand in front of this three way mirror in your slip. You suck it in in the front, and it sticks out in the back. That is displaying your size.

DOS: That's the one between uno and tres.

DUMP: Anybody who has ever worked in a school knows what dump is. That's when the principal brings all this stack of stuff and dumps it on your desk at 4 p.m. and wants it before you leave.

FLUTTER: That's what you do with your eyelashes.

HORIZONTAL RESOLUTION: I figured out that is a decision you make in bed.

PREROLL: This is where you buy your cigarettes in a package instead of rolling them from a sack of Bull Durham or pot.

SHOTGUN: Everybody knows what a shotgun is. It's what you hang on that gun rack on the back of your pick-me-up truck.

SUPERIMPOSITION: That's when you take a friend to the grocery store, and then when

you get there she wants to go the library and
the bank and to check on her mother.
The acronym I remember the best has come from people
who have tried to teach me how to use the computer.
They just say to me, "Oh, R-T-F-M, and walk out" --- or
Read the F....ing Manual.

WHERE HAVE ALL THE GOOD TEXAS
EDUCATORS GONE...
LONG TIME PASSING?...

WHERE HAVE ALL THE GOOD TEXAS
EDUCATORS GONE...
LONG TIME AGO?...

While royal families learned centuries ago that too
much inbreeding begat idiots, I am still concerned that
almost every time a vacancy occurs in the public schools
of Texas -- from the superintendent to the assistant custo-
dian in the bus barn -- a consultant is hired and a
NATIONAL SEARCH is instigated.

What has suddenly become so wrong with promoting

someone who is already in the district (many times in the same building where the vacancy occurs), is doing a good job, is loved and respected for personal, professional, and leadership qualities by students, faculty, and parents; and would make the transition easy, fast, and relatively inexpensive? Why do we automatically assume that a person who is doing a fantastic job in Public School #579 in New York City will be a perfect fit as principal of the elementary school in Cross Plains, Texas? Why is far away always better?

I think even kings sometimes wished they had married their fifth cousin twice removed rather that the Princess of Outer Mongolia...at least Cousin Beatrice would have known the family.

Probably all of us who have been in education most of our lives have been in schools with a few good ol' boys and good ol' girls with great big mouths and little-bitty brains who were durn near impossible to hide except in the Central Office. But we have also worked with truly great educators who had come up through the ranks, if not in their own districts, from somewhere close enough for us to drive over and visit. They came in every shape and size, race and color, sex and age. They all had as their common denominator the true belief that schools were created for the kids so each and every one of them would have the best and safest environment in which to learn and reach their highest potential in every way. These true educators knew schools were not created so that we would have jobs, or so the legislature could meet ever two years and fight over the budget (money for schools vs. money for prisons), or even so companies could sell computers. Schools were created for kids.

We sit around on our apathy and bemoan the fact that the best and brightest are leaving the field of education or else not entering it. And yet, what should we expect when they have to take an additional job to support their families and have little hope that doing a good job, paying their dues, and being truly outstanding will be recognized where they are, much less rewarded? Where is the affirmation?

Where have all the good Texas educators gone? Perhaps to New Jersey where they were picked up by a NATIONAL SEARCH.

PRINCIPAL STORIES....

I really do love most principals, but I have all these great principal stories that all the teachers just love, so principals, I'm going to give you a hard time--just bear with me. Principals really are the most important people in the school building. They set the tone for the whole school. I can walk in a building and tell you what the principal is like. Here are a few stories about principals.

WHO'S IN CHARGE OF THE GRADE BOOKS?

We had this new principal who pulled on his lapels a lot and was very territorial ....The first trait was obvious: the second I learned the hard way.

Soon after school started in August one of the teachers came by my office to say she needed a grade book but had to rush to class and wondered if I would pick one up from the principal's office and send it to her room. I assured her this would be not problem--little did I know.

I strolled to the principal's arena and told his secretary, who had been at the school for a number of years, that I needed to pick up a grade book. In her innocence or ignorance of the present administration, she stood up, opened the top drawer of the filing cabinet and said, "Sure...no problem." Little did she know.

Faster than a speeding bullet, the principal shot out of his office, pushed the file drawer closed (barely missing the well-manicured finger of the secretary), pulled on his lapels, froze me with an icy stare and stated in no uncertain terms, "You don't give grades!"

To which I stammered, "I know I don't, but I was getting a grade book for a teacher."

He flinched, got a little red in the face, gave an emphatic yank to his lapels and declared, "I'm in charge of the grade books."

"*What*?" I gasped.

"I'm in charge of the grade books!" he declared loudly.

Still in a state of shock, I ventured, "What did you say?"

Leaning forward, fixing me with a stare that made the first icy one seem like a heat wave, pulling on his lapels with all his might, he roared, "*I said I'm in charge of the grade books!*"

Knowing when to hold 'em and when to fold 'em, I turned to make a hasty retreat, muttering to myself, "That's about your speed." Thank God he didn't hear me, but he pursued me just the same, grabbed my arm, pulled me into his office, and added to my horror by closing the door. He then proceeded to the big chair behind his big desk, sat down, and with a downward flick of his index finger indicated I was also to be seated. I sat, feeling like a freshman who had just set off a stink bomb in the hall, and waited for the ax to fall.

He leaned across his desk, pulled on his lapels, and inquired in the intimidating voice of Perry Mason, *"**Who doesn't know I'm in charge of the grade books?**"*

Willing to do anything or say anything to get from behind the closed door, I said in the most humble voice of my life, "I don't know who **doesn't**, but I **do**. And I bet you do the best job handing out grade books of anybody in the world, but could Mrs. Durr have a grade book?"

Obviously relieved and a little pleased with my compliment, he gave a kinder, gentler pull to his lapels, and said, "Yes...if she'll come in here so she knows who's in charge of the grade books."

I gave him a shaky smile and rushed out of the door while I was still ahead. From the lion's den, I went directly to my counseling office where I called all the counselors and secretary in, closed the door, looked them right in the eye and asked, "Do you know who's in charge of the grade books?"

Those fools asked in unison, *"**Who cares?**"*

I shook my arthritic finger in their faces and admonished, "Watch it! I'm going to tell you who cares and don't you ever forget it!"

I used to think this was the worst kind of principal in the world to have, but it isn't. The worst kind in the world to have is the one who doesn't know **what** he's in charge of.

THEY CAN'T COME BACK FROM WHERE THEY'VE NEVER BEEN

You run into some principals who are wonderful! Charlie Thomas at Nederland, Texas was a wonderful principal. We got paid every two weeks and every two weeks he took the checks around to everyone in his building. He always said to me (and I understood later he said to everybody), "Toody Fay, this is not nearly enough money for what you do for us. If it were in my power, I'd give you ten times this much money. You are wonderful!! What you do for our kids -- there's no way to pay you."

You know, I went to work at daylight; I stayed 'til dark. I'm sure that man might have been able to ask me something I wouldn't have done--if it was immoral, I'd have had to think about it a little bit. As I think back, I don't think the man ever did get me a raise, but I believe to my soul today that he would have if he could.

What we as teachers want is for principals to brag on us. Well--with most of them--<u>forget that</u>! You know, they can't come back from where they've never been! And who brags on principals? We've learned to brag on kids. That makes them do better. And sometimes as teachers, we get so desperate for praise that we praise each other. But who brags on principals? When they're not doing a good job, we talk about them in the lounge. When they are, we figure it's no more than they ought to be doing-- they're getting paid for it.

So teachers, brag on your principals -- even if you have to make it up!

THE PAPER SHORTAGE

For teachers who are brand new, you haven't dealt with this principal, but any of us who have had at least five years of experience have had at least one of these -- that is the principal who's worried about the "paper short- age." You know, I don't know how much paper costs, but

I know it costs more than the career ladder ... and buses...and football equipment, because they talk about it so much.

And when you've got a principal worried about the paper shortage, I think certain people evolve within the faculty. There is one I call the "Keeper of the Quota." She has this little black book--I never have figured out when this woman teaches because she always keeps up with everything else so well--but she gets up after the principal has talked about the paper shortage, opens the black book and declares, "I think it ought to be brought to the attention of the faculty that Mr. Montgomery has used his quota of paper through April, and it is only October."

Well, Mr. Montgomery is the band director, and he jumps straight up and he says, "Listen here, I want to tell you something! They won't give me enough money to buy all the music I need, and I'm in the spotlight every Friday night, and I've got to use that Xerox paper for the music."

She shrugs, smiles smugly, and counters with, "All I know is you have used your quota through April, and it is only October. **Do not think you are going to get any of the quota of the Social Studies Department.**"

And then you always have this one--she is usually a "young" woman about my age and weight--who stands up, with the piety of Tammy Faye, raises her eyebrows innocently, and says, "I haven't used **any** paper. I'm just trying to do what the principal asked. I'm writing everything on the board." (The young teachers in the back are just giving her the finger - they're so mad they could just kill her.)

A few years ago, we had this principal who was just great, but we had a million problems that year. About November, we went into a faculty meeting and of all the dumb things, he got started on the paper shortage. Walking back to the office I said, "Pat, with all the other problems we have, why in the hell did you get started on the paper shortage?"

"All right, Miss Smarty," he said, "Just tell me, what we're going to do when March comes around and there is no paper and there is no money to buy any? What do you expect me to do?"

"Well, Pat," I informed him, "you'll just have to sell your truck."

I want you to understand that I thought that was a lot funnier than Pat did.

KEEPER OF THE QUOTA

TEACHERS ARE THE DREAMERS OF THE WORLD!

I think we, as educators, especially need to hold on to our dreams and help kids hold on to theirs, because we are the romantics of the world. We're the dreamers. We see these kids not only as they are, but as they can be. We need to give them a vision of greatness.....A vision that says, "Don't believe everything you read or see on TV-- this is really a wonderful world and you have an important place in it."

And we're so in need of dreams now. I don't think anything brought this home closer than the tragedy of the Challenger. That happened years ago, but every time someone goes up in space, the media talks about the Challenger. I think this is because of Christa. You know, she wasn't really the first civilian in space; she was just the first one everybody could identify with. First, because she was a teacher, but more than that because she had a dream, and she talked about it a lot. She called it reaching for the stars, and we got caught up in it. High schoolers wanted TV's in their rooms to see the blast off. People waiting on bus corners got caught up in it, so her dream became our dream, and her tragedy became our tragedy.

But her hope is our hope.

I don't care if you reach for the stars with Christa, or if you say with King Arthur, "Don't let it be forgot that once there was a spot that for one brief shining moment was known as Camelot." There are stars to be reached, and Camelots to be found, and you'll find them, and you'll help these kids find them. And if we all work together, maybe--just maybe--we may be able to create a new generation of kids whose heroes are parents and teachers instead of movie stars and professional athletes. Good luck!

FIRST MAJOR BIAS: TEACHING OR WORKING WITH KIDS IS THE MOST EXCITING THING IN THE WORLD AND THE MOST IMPORTANT

Through the years, I've developed some major biases--and all of us are biased. Anytime someone says to me that he or she has a completely unbiased opinion about someone or something, if it's one of my good days, I say "B.S.," because none of us are completely unbiased. The first major bias I have is that teaching or working with kids is the most exciting thing in the world and the most important. The bumper sticker I like best is the one, "If you can read this, thank a teacher," because I never watch on TV or hear on the radio or read in the newspaper about a Nobel Prize winner or somebody who has done something great that my first thought is not, "Some teacher taught that kid to read, and some other teacher inspired him to study math or science or whatever." What could be more important than that? You know, how many open heart surgeries can the best heart surgeon do in a lifetime, but as teachers we can reach from 22 to 150 kids every day and make a difference. What could be more important than that?

But somewhere along the way we forgot to stand up and be counted, and I'm a great believer that "he who tooteth not his own horn, the same is not tooteth." We need to talk about the great job we do. We need to say to our kids, "You've done a wonderful job of learning, and look how much I helped you--go home and tell your mamas!" Sometimes, I think if we are downtrodden, it's because we've downtrodden ourselves. I also think some of the changes that have come about that have scared us so, we asked for, because somewhere in the course of the years we got so caught up in higher salaries, better benefits--and God knows, I'm not knocking it because we needed them--that we forgot to say we are proud to be teachers.

I'd go to parties and meet somebody and ask, "What do you do?" She'd glance around to be sure nobody was looking and listening, then she'd say, "Oh, I'm just a teacher." Or worse yet, "I'm just an elementary teacher." **This is where it is.** You don't hear doctors going around saying, "Oh, I'm just a doctor." You don't even hear doctors' wives say, "Oh, I'm just a doctor's wife." And you certainly don't hear a lawyer say, "Oh, I'm just a lawyer." They say, "I am an attorney." (They used to be lawyers.) But we forgot to say we are teachers and be proud of it.

As teachers, if we judge our worth by our salaries or our prestige in the community, we are always going to be disappointed. We need to judge our worth on how many kids smile when they come into our class or say "Aw" when the bell rings at the end of the period; we need to judge it on how many kids in the fourth grade come back to see their third grade teacher or call us from who knows where fifteen or twenty years after they leave our classes. That's why schools were created and that's why teachers are so important. So teachers, stand up and be counted!

TO WILLIAM, THE READER FROM MRS. NEWMAN, THE TEACHER

One of my favorite speakers is William Purkey, and this is one of my favorite stories he tells about his reading teacher in the sixth grade, Mrs. Newman. He said every time Mrs. Newman had a kid who didn't or wouldn't or couldn't read, she'd call his/her name and say, "Come up here, I want to give you a present." And he said she'd reach back and get an old flea-bitten book out of this old bookcase, and she'd write, "To William(or whatever the child's name was), the Reader, from Mrs. Newman, the Teacher." As he said, how would you not go home and read something that had been given to you, the Reader, by Mrs. Newman, the Teacher?

William Purkey goes on, "You know, I'm kind of a slow learner. I got to college before it occurred to me that Mrs. Newman gave away ten or fifteen books every day, and there was never a vacant spot in that old bookcase." So he called her and asked, "Mrs. Newman, I've begun to wonder about your never-ending supply of books."

She said, "It took you long enough to wonder, William, but if you'll pick me up in the morning, I'll show you how I'm doing this." The next morning he picked her up at 8 o'clock, and they drove around to all the yard sales. When she would see books, she'd say, "Stop the car, William." He'd stop the car and she would get out, walk up to the owners and say, "I am a teacher. You ought to **give** me those books."

William reports, "I never saw her not get every book that they had and I never saw her pay a penny for it."

The key word was TEACHER. I am a TEACHER. You ought to give me those books.

I'M A TEACHER AND YOU KNOW BETTER THAN THAT!

We had a sweet, young teacher at our school named Rosiemerry, and she and her husband saved enough money to take a trip to Greece. In order to save more money, they went on a ship, and in order to save even more money, Bobby stayed with the men and Rosiemerry stayed with the other women. She said that one night she went to bed before anyone else, and something awakened her. Here was this man going through her purse.

Now, Rosiemerry is this cute little thing, but she

said, "I just went crazy! I thought, this may be the only vacation we can ever take like this, and every penny of spending money we have is in my purse." She said she sat straight up in bed and using her sternest voice, said, "You put that down. I am a **teacher**, and you know better than that!"

He dropped the purse and said, "Yes, maam" and then ran out.

I don't know if you teachers ought to try that on some of these punks now, but it worked for Rosiemerry.

GIVE YOURSELF A GIFT -- VISIT A KINDERGARTEN CLASS

I don't care how old your kids are. Give yourselves the gift of visiting a kindergarten class once a year. It'll change your whole outlook on life. I walked into a kindergarten class one Friday afternoon, and this little boy came up to me and asked, "Who are you and what are you doing here?" I thought this was absolutely wonderful, because this is what every kid, "K" through graduate school, wants to know when somebody they don't know walks into the room--but it's only in kindergarten where we haven't squelched them so much that they are afraid to

ask.   So, I told him who I was and why I was there, and
he said, "O.K., so why don't you stay a while."

In a little bit, he came back to me and said, "Hey, I
wish you had been here yesterday, Lady. We did a spear-
ment."

"What kind of experiment did you do?"

"Spearmint," he said.

I said, "O.K., what kind of spearmint did you do?"

With his little-boy-clean thumb pointed toward the
floor, he announced, "Sink," then immediately stuck his
"pointer" finger toward the ceiling and said, "'Float' that's
a concept."

"What did you do?" I asked.

He explained, "We made some jello, and we put
some fruit in it. The fruit that was heavier than the jello
sank." He pointed down again and said, "Heavy--sink."
He went on, "The fruit that was lighter than the jello float-
ed. Light--float." He repeated the words and motions,
"Heavy--sink. Light--float. Heavy--sink. Light--float.
That's a concept." He elbowed me in the side and said,
"Got it?"

"I got it. I got it," I said as I rubbed my side.

Just before the bell rang, I saw him say something to
his teacher and then run over to me. He asked me, "You

want a 'cause sticker?"

I said, " Sure. What's a 'cause sticker?"

"Well," he said, "every Friday-- it don't make any difference how much bad stuff we've done all week--our teacher gives us a sticker 'cause she loves us."

I thought, "Isn't that wonderful?" I went back by my superintendent's office and said, "I want to tell you about something--I want you to give me a 'cause sticker every Friday--no matter how much bad stuff I've done all week." He just sighed, shook his head, and said, " You really almost lose it sometimes, don't you, Toody!"

But I think that was a marvelous lesson. I think we ought to hand out 'cause stickers of one kind or another to our kids as long as we have them.

KIDS, NOT MOTHERS,
LOVE KINDERGARTEN TEACHERS

For those of you who are kindergarten teachers, do not expect the mothers of the kindergarten children--especially if they're the first or only child--to love you. You know, I learned to hate my kids' first grade teachers. The only reason I didn't hate their kindergarten teachers is that they didn't go to kindergarten. But here I was, I had been the most important woman in those kids' lives for six years, and suddenly, they were with somebody else.

My daughter was obviously a gifted and talented child. It took her just three days to replace me with the teacher. That kid was quite assertive--just like her daddy-- and she didn't want to drink milk. I made her drink milk every morning and every night. But, in the first grade, she just had thirty minutes at home at noon for lunch, and I didn't want to fight it, so I just gave her tea, so she'd drink it and get back to school. The third day she walked in, pointed to the glass and, in a horrified voice, asked, "What is this in this glass?"

"Well, it's tea, Judy, you have it every day at noon," I said.

She put the back of her hand to her forehead, rolled her eyes to the ceiling, then fixed me with a glare worthy of a teenager and said, " My teacher, Mrs. Jones, says growing children should have milk three times a day."

You know, just like I was trying to poison her!

Then her brother, Alan Byrd, was alone for two years after Judy started school, and we got to be really close friends, and we loved each other. When he started school, he was a slower learner--it took him a whole week to replace me.

He came home on Friday and said, "Mama, I wish you looked more like my teacher, Miss Parnell."

Well, hell! Miss Parnell looked **then** about like I do **now**, and I was young and cute. I learned to really hate that big, old, fat woman.

So, kindergarten teachers, just accept that the kids love you and go on from there.

THIGHS AND NOSES

For those of you who work with little kids, you need to remember that if little kids stand up when you stand up, they stand up in a world of adult thighs. And, if they sit down and you stand up right above them and they look up, they look up into a world of adult noses. Thighs and noses--and neither of those things is too enticing.

I used to tell our personnel director, if you are looking for elementary teachers, one of the things you always need to do is see how easily their knees bend because we frown on little kids getting up on things and still--if they don't get up, and we don't get down, it's thighs and noses.

I can remember in the first grade that this principal

of ours had the longest dadgum nose you can imagine. I can remember his walking over and putting his hand on my shoulder (I'm sure he was just picking on me, because I was a model child) and saying, "Toody, look up here at me!"

Oh! I just couldn't bring myself to.

And then he'd pinch my shoulders and say, "Do not be insubordinate!"

Insubordinate is a good first grade word. I didn't know what the hell it meant, but I knew it had to do with noses.

Remember...Thighs and Noses.

WHAT IS A MIDDLE SCHOOLER?

A middle schooler is a different breed of cat. I used to love middle school. I used to swear if I had 25 kids for 45 minutes, I could deal with 150 different personalities. I found something I thought you might like. I have no idea who wrote it--wish I had:

What is a Middle Schooler?

What is a middle schooler? I was asked one day.

I knew what it was, but what could I say?

He's noise and confusion; he's silence that's deep.

He's sunshine and laughter, or a cloud that will weep.

He's as swift as an arrow; he's a waster of time.

He wants to be rich, but he can't save a dime.

He's rude and nasty; he's as polite as can be.

He wants parental guidance, but he fights to be free.

He's aggressive and bossy; he's timid and shy.

He knows all the answers, but still he asks, "Why?"

He's awkward and clumsy; he's graceful and poised.

He's ever-changing--but don't be annoyed.

What is a middle schooler? I was asked one day.

He's the future unfolding -- Don't get in his way!

SCARLETT, YOU REALLY ARE A BITCH!

I've always thought that Prissy was the most believable character in Gone with the Wind because she was this typical young teenager. I must have seen Gone with the Wind fifteen times, and I still can't understand how Scarlett could hang on to that asinine Ashley Wilkes when Rhett Butler was waiting in the wings. I also thought that

if I watched that show enough times, one night Melanie
was going to say, "You know, Scarlett, you really <u>are</u> a
bitch!"

But the one you can always depend on, who is just
typical and perfect in her role, is Prissy. Here's Atlanta
blowing up all around her, blood and guts everywhere, and
she's walking along this picket fence in her other world.
The fact that she told somebody just an hour ago that she
knew all about "birthing babies"--and now she doesn't
know anything--doesn't bother her; that was an hour ago.

But, young teenagers are also wonderful. It's the last
time we get them before their guard is up.

THERE IS NO HURRY

Let me tell you elementary teachers one thing that
you do better than anybody else in the world: you are the
best "Stoppers of Runners." I have never passed an elementary school where kids are coming in from recess or
P.E., or whatever, that the kids can't wait to get back in--
they're just charging. Not so the teachers--It's **"Slow
down. Do not run. Walk. There is no hurry. Line up.
Do not run. There is no hurry."**

Teachers, if you don't think you've taught that lesson, you ought to come to the high school. Between every class we're in the halls saying, "Hurry up. Get to class. You're going to be late. You're going to be late! Don't kiss her again--Go on. Go on." You've programmed them too early, too well. <u>There is no hurry</u>. But elementary teachers, you're the beginning--you're what makes them tick.

TEACHERS' APPRAISALS AND A CULMINATING ACTIVITY

I think we should take a clue from Judge Roy Bean. Do you know how Judge Roy Bean got to be the "Law West of the Pecos"? He <u>said</u> he was the Law West of the Pecos. We are good teachers -- we need to be going around saying it. I think that is one of the reasons we've lost some of our status.

Another of the reasons is that we haven't policed our own very well. You know, we've all been in schools where we've had "good ol' girls" and "good ol' boys" who have great big mouths and little bitty brains--and they are durn near impossible to hide. I think the formal appraisal system we now face is due to this failure to police our own.

I have had trouble with the appraisal system from the beginning. Our superintendent asked me one time, "Toody, what do you think about the appraisal system?"

I told him, "I think it just scares the hell out of our good teachers, and our bad teachers have blown it off like they do everything else."

But I want to tell you this story about the appraisal system--it's not very nice, but it's true, and it's real funny.

When appraisals first began, one of our math teachers had already had her first appraisal visit, and she was out in the hall when the typing teacher came up to her and said she was "next."

"Tell me, tell me, what to do! Tell me how I can get some EQ's and get on the career ladder," she said.

"Well," the math teacher advised, "I'll tell you something. One thing that is really important is that you have a good culminating activity. It's good to ask some questions, preferably ones that the kids can answer."

"But I teach typing," the business teacher said. "We've been going six weeks. What possible questions could the kids have?" And then she began to smile and said, "Oh, I know what I'll do. I'll plant two kids in my class, and I'll have one raise his hand and ask, "Miss Miller, which finger do you hit the *D* key with?"

She said, raising her middle finger, I'll say, "This one."

"Then I'll plant this other one, and he'll say, 'Mrs. Miller, which finger do you hit the *K* key with?'"

And, raising her other middle finger, she said, "I'll say, 'This one.'"

"And then," she said, "I'll hold both hands up and smile and say, 'This is my culminating activity.'"

You know, I breathed a sigh of relief and thought, "We may be down, but we ain't out." We are going to laugh and go on.

REMINDER FOR TEACHERS' APPRAISERS

I want to tell you appraisers a story about this one teacher who was involved in a situation we had at school a few years ago that scared us all to death. This kid came to the high school with a loaded gun (before it was the "in" thing to do). He was running around all over school with it, and nobody could get the gun--nobody was even attempting to.

Finally, someone took the gun away from him, and they brought the kid to the principal's office. This establishes pecking order--the principal takes the kid's parents into his office to talk about it, and he leaves me with the kid who had had the gun. This is the maddest kid that I have ever seen! He's sitting there shaking, with his fists doubled up, and he's gritting his teeth. I'm trying to talk to him about the gun, and every little bit he jumps up and runs out. And I jump up and chase him. Well, five times after I've jumped up and chased him, I think: <u>one</u> of us really does have a problem.   So the next time he runs out, I just sit there and in a little while he comes back in, because he doesn't have any place to go. He sits back down, and I decide I'm not going to even try to talk about the gun--I'm just going to try to get him relaxed. So, as a well-trained counselor, this is what I do: Now, here is this kid mad enough at the system to kill somebody, and I'm going to pass the time of day with him. I say, "Bryan, what courses are you taking?"

Well, he goes all to pieces and he growls, "Old Lady (he had been calling me that all along), let me tell you what courses I'm taking." And he starts going through them one at a time, telling me how he hates the teachers, etc.

You know, the first thing you learn to do as a counselor is be evasive. And the next thing is to be a real good
listener, and so I listened to him and realized he hadn't
told me but about five classes. So, I said, "Bryan, who do
you have physical science with?"

I wish you could have seen that kid! He became a
different person. He unclenched his hands, and he leaned
back in his chair and said, "Oh, Mrs. Byrd, I have Coach
Reed and he is wonderful!"

"You know, he's the one who took the gun away
from me," he said. "I was running up and down the hall,
scared to death, wishing somebody would take the gun
away from me. The doors would open, and they would
look out and rush back and slam the doors."

"Somebody must have alerted Coach Reed," he said,
"because when I got to his door, he came out and stopped
in front of me and said, 'Bryan, what are you doing with
that gun? Let me have it. <u>Friends</u> don't need guns.'"

Bryan said, "I gave it to him, because friends don't
need guns. You know, Mrs. Byrd, Coach Reed is the
greatest man in the world. He likes me better than anybody in school. The other kids in his class think he likes
them best, but he likes me best. Every day, he puts his
arm around my shoulder and says, 'Boy, you have made

my day, being here.' Oh, Mrs. Byrd," he said, "he's the only reason I come to school."

And for the next thirty minutes, this kid told me all he had learned in physical science. He told me a whole lot more about physical science than I ever wanted to know. But, when he got through, he said, "Let's do what we have to do about the gun, and then I need to go talk this over with Coach Reed."

You know, I don't know if Jerry Reed is going to get on the career ladder. I don't know that he gets a bunch of EQ's. I just know he happens to be the kind of guy that takes guns away from friends and keeps kids in school. I hope we won't forget him in the appraisal process.

A SECOND BIAS:
TEACHERS AND ADMINISTRATORS ARE THE
MOST IMPORTANT PEOPLE IN A KID'S LIFE
WHILE HE IS IN SCHOOL

A second bias I have is that teachers and administrators, especially teachers, are the most important people in kids' lives while they are in school. I do not believe schools were created so the legislatures could get together and argue over money (money for schools and money for prisons, without ever seeing the connection). They were not created to sell yellow school buses. They were not made so that publishing companies could make a mint of money publishing textbooks with a bunch of mistakes in them. They were not even created to give teachers jobs. Schools were created for kids...so they'd have the safest and the best and the most exciting and the most caring place to be during the hours of their days. And for these kids, the most important people in their lives at school are the teachers and administrators. Think about it. What do you remember about school? The buildings? The overlays on the overhead projector? Now, I know this will be blasphemy for you elementary teachers, but I bet you don't even remember the bulletin boards.

You remember the teachers. And, Teachers, if you don't think you're important, I wish you could read the follow-ups that I did on our graduates every six years. The one question that every kid answered on the survey--and sometimes this was the only one that he did answer--was "who or what influenced you most when you were in school?" Every kid answered that question, and every kid put the name of a teacher. I never left them any room to write because I knew what they would do. Sure enough, they always put a little star and wrote, "Look on the back." Not only did they want to tell me the name of the teacher, they wanted to tell me something about him/her.

One of them wrote, "Mr. McGill influenced me the most. When I was in his seventh grade science class, I was 6', weighed 100 pounds, had long skinny legs, size 12 feet, and bumps all over my face. I knew I was stupid because I looked so bad. I just walked around and recognized people by their belt buckles. I hated school, and I hated science. One time I turned in a test paper, and I hadn't done very well on it, but Mr. McGill had put the grade and then he had written, 'Look on the back page.' I flipped over to the back page and Mr. McGill had written, 'Don't worry about being 6' and weighing 100 pounds in the seventh grade, with skinny legs and bumps all over your face. I looked just like you do when I was your age, and look how handsome I am today.'"

"From that point on," the student said, "the way I looked seemed less important, and science and Mr. McGill seemed more important. I straightened myself up and actually saw faces...and I became smarter." He went on, "Just for the record, Mrs. Byrd, I'm teaching science now in junior high, just like Mr. McGill."

Another one recalled, "Mrs. Atwood influenced me

the most. I was there during the hippy era, and I looked bad and smelled worse. She looked good and smelled good, and patted me anyway."

And then, always at least one, but usually ten or twenty kids, put the name of Mary Lou Heard as the person who had influenced them the most. Mary Lou Heard had taught fifth grade social studies for 142 years at our school, and every kid who put her name down, put exactly the same thing. They said, "Mrs. Heard believed in me when nobody else did."

Don't kid yourself that you're not the most important thing in the kids' lives when they are at school.

A THIRD BIAS: THE WORLD IS MADE UP OF TWO KINDS OF PEOPLE: PEOPLE PEOPLE AND THINGS PEOPLE

A third bias I have is that the world is made up of two kinds of people: People People and Things People. People People ought to work with people. We ought to be teachers. We ought to be coaches. We ought to sell things in stores. Things People ought to work on computers in the back of banks. They ought to fix car motors. They ought to put roofs on houses. There is a real need for both kinds of people, but the unhappiest adults I deal with are People People in Things People jobs and Things People in People People jobs!   You can spot them a mile off.

I went in the Taco Bell the other night and this kid walks up and blurts out, "Whadja want?"

I jumped about a foot high and stammered, "Ah...a...hamburger?"

She glared at me and said, "At the *Taco* Bell???"

Eager to make amends, I said, " A taco."

She leaned over, pointed her finger straight at my nose and said, "Just one??"

I leaned away from the threatening finger, bit my bottom lip, held up two fingers and said, "Three."

But what I thought was, "Honey, you ought to be in the back room making those tacos, and let some People People be up here selling them. We'd both feel better."

But every once in a while you get people who fit. We had to have a new roof put on our house, and I pulled into the driveway and this guy was putting these shingles on. It was 105 in the shade, and I got out and said, "Hello."

He didn't answer me...just kept putting the shingles on.

"Wouldn't you like me to get you something cool to drink?" I asked politely.

He didn't answer me....just kept putting the shingles on.

Well, I climbed the ladder! And I want you to know that I think a big ol' Coke will raise the dead. And so I got up there by him and said, "Mister, wouldn't you like for me to get you a Coke?"

"Lady," he said, "what I'd really like for you to do is leave me alone so I can put these shingles on."

The Big Byrd was standing down on the ground laughing. "Hey, Toody," he said, "that's a Things People in a Things People job...leave him alone."

But you know, every once in a while you find in a school Things People in the People People job of teaching, and they are miserable. You can spot them. Kids can spot them in ten minutes. I had a kid come in once and say, "You know, Mrs. Smith hates kids."

In my best counselor's manner, I said, "Oh, she never **said** that to me."

"No," he said, "she never has said it to me either, but I know it."

"How do you know?" I asked.

"Because," he explained, "between classes she stands out in the hall talking to the other teachers, and she looks so

relaxed and is having a good time. The bell rings, and she moves and stands in the door with her arms folded across her chest and glares. Then she calls the roll and looks up between the names and just dares us to be present. And then she will get to working these problems on the board. I sit over to the side, and can see that she gets so relaxed and is smiling. Then one of us idiots asks a question, and she turns around, glares, and says "What?? (loud and clear)."

"I think she likes to teach," he reasoned. "I think she's just sorry that it has to be to kids."

I think he's right.

If you happen to be one of those Things People in a Peoples People job like teaching, GET OUT. You know, chances are you're never going to get rich anyway, and there are easier ways to lose your mind.

ANOTHER MAJOR BIAS: CARING ABOUT KIDS IS THE MOST IMPORTANT ATTRIBUTE YOU CAN HAVE AS A TEACHER

Another major bias I have is this: Caring about kids is the most important attribute you can have as a teacher.

There is not one thing in any course you take or in any textbook that tells you this. And still, if you don't have it, you can get as many degrees as you have the time and inclination and money to get; you can develop the best skills; you can design the best possible program; you can be the best technical and most efficient teacher in the world; you can get your Phi Beta Kappa pin tattooed to your forehead; you can go to every method workshop that is offered, and you may get to be a good technician, but you are never going to be a great teacher if you don't care. Because--trust me--**kids do not care how much you know until they know how much you care. And, if you can't reach them, you can't teach them.**

WE ARE PREDISPOSED TO LIKE SOME KIDS BETTER THAT OTHERS

Carl Pickhardt, a psychologist and great friend of mine, did the best workshop I ever attended. In addition to being a psychologist, he is also a cartoonist. He drew these caricatures of four kids -- the hostile kid, the "poor me" kid, the apathetic kid, and the super-intelligent kid. There were about 100 counselors there, and he told us to go stand by the kids we'd want to work with the most. I like hostility. I thought everyone would go stand by the hostile kid. Not so. We were almost equally divided into four groups. He gave us this big sheet of paper and had us describe the kid we had chosen. And we did-- we just wrote and wrote.

Then he had all of us go stand by the kid we'd want to work with the least. I thought everybody would go stand by the "poor me." I have a hard time with these kids. But again, we were about equally divided. He had us describe this kid, and we did.

Then he said, "Now, we have two descriptions of the same kid." You would never have recognized the two descriptions as the same kid. It was a remarkable revelation. He said, "I think you should recognize that when you like a kid, you see all these positive things about him. When you don't like a kid, you see all the negatives. You need to face that no matter what we say, none of us is really unbiased. You need to recognize what is happening to you and deal with it. If you have another counselor who likes to work with that kind of kid, give that kid to her, because you aren't going to do him any good."

It's the same way with teachers. We had these LST's (local support team) where we'd get all the teachers in to talk about a kid. You'd have six teachers, and I never had an LST where at least one teacher didn't think that kid was wonderful. They'd be talking about the good things about this kid that none of the rest of us had ever seen.

We see what we are predisposed to see.

"MEEZ, YOU DON'T KNOW NOTHING ABOUT PUTTING TOGETHER CHRISTMAS TREES!"

You don't always have to be right. Kids think you are perfect enough anyway. I had one dad who would call me every Monday morning and say, "I was right about what I said about Ben; I was right!" (And he was.)

Finally, one day I said to him, "Why would you always rather be *right* than *loved*?"

You don't have to always be right.

When I was teaching in Austin, I had this kid, Rudy, who really seemed slow. This was before it was mandated that you couldn't move kids along when they were older and bigger than anybody else. So, Rudy had been moved along, and he was probably about seventeen when I got him for 9th grade world geography.

Every day I'd go by his desk and try to help him, and he'd just look daggers at me and say, "Go away, *'Meez,'* I don't need no help."

Then every day after school was out, my door would open and in would come Rudy. He would say, *"Meez,* I'm coming in to spend some time with you 'cause I don't like you."

I'd say, "Come on in, Rudy, 'cause I don't like you either."

So, we'd spend an extra 45 minutes to an hour together every afternoon 'cause we didn't like each other. We talked about everything from "shootin' up" to being nice to your mother, but he would never let me help him with his school work.

Just before Christmas, I brought this old aluminum Christmas tree to school to put up in my room. I was putting that tree together, and as you know, they are pretty easy to put together--they've got these slanted notches. Then I thought, " I believe I'll see if Rudy can do any-thing."

So, I twisted those limbs and turned them upside down and looked at them, puzzled. Rudy was just about to have a fit watching me. He finally jerked those limbs out of my hands and said, "Meez, you don't know nothing about putting together Christmas trees." He started putting those branches in the notches and had it together in nothing flat. He put it on its stand and said again, "Meez, you don't know nothing about putting together Christmas trees. You're a teacher, and you can't even put together a Christmas tree. You know, if it was up to you, we probably wouldn't even have a Christmas tree up here."

I agreed that he was right. So, we had the Christmas party and left for Christmas vacation. When we got back to school after the holidays, we were having world geography, and I gave them all a map--Rudy didn't work on it. I tried to help him, but he said, "Get away, Meez, I don't need no help."

I shrugged my shoulders and said, "Suits me, but it seems to me that some people can put together Christmas trees, and some people can do world geography."

I walked to the back of the room, and in a little bit he motioned for me to come up to him. I went up to his desk, and he looked at me and whispered, "You don't know nothing about putting together Christmas trees. If it hadn't been for me, we probably wouldn't have even had a Christmas tree. I really did help you."

"That's right, Rudy," I said.

He said quietly, "I really don't know nothing about

world geography, but I really did help you with that Christmas tree, didn't I?" I agreed that he had.

"So, maybe you can help me with this world geography," he said. So I did help him, and he did real well.

And things changed in our after-school visits, too: he began to let me help him with his courses. I knew all the time he was smart because he was so street-wise and so articulate, but he couldn't read well enough to follow written directions--so he just didn't do anything. We began to work on reading and math and science and social studies, and our one hour after school turned into two and sometimes three. But Rudy learned. And at the end of the semester, he passed all his courses for the first time since third grade. I do think the principal thought I was stretching the point when I gave him an A+ in World Geography, but I thought that was between Rudy and me.

Well, Rudy didn't finish high school. He went to Vietnam. I got this letter from him:

Dear Mrs. Byrd,
Hope you are well. Blessed be to God. We got this
new dumb a...lieutenant. (I wish you could have seen
how he spelled lieutenant.) *This Dumb A...don't*
know nothing about guerrilla warfare (He spelled

guerrilla just about the way he spelled lieutenant.)
and he won't let me help him. He ought to know that
anybody who's come from East Austin knows a lot
about guerrilla warfare even if they've never been in the
army, but he won't let me help him. He's going
to get us all killed, cause the Dumb A... never has
learned that some people can put together Christmas
trees and some people can do world geography.

Love,

Rudy

Well, Rudy didn't come back from Vietnam. That letter is
one of the treasures of my life. Ever so often I read it to
remember I'm not that smart and we don't always have to
be right, and Rudy knew at one time he could do something
better than anyone else--even the teacher.

KIDS HAVE TAUGHT ME SO MUCH

All kids, especially the "at-risk" ones, have taught me
so much. One day I broke my glasses. I am as blind as a
bat without my glasses, and I just went crazy. The next day,
Gregory came to class and said, "Mrs. Byrd, let me tell

you something about what you did yesterday. You were so mean when you broke your glasses. You yelled at us, and you had never yelled at us in your life. We came up and hovered around like we always do and you said, ' Get back! Get back.' And finally, I got up right in your face so you'd see me and you pushed me. You know, Mrs. Byrd, you weren't mad at us; you were mad because you couldn't see--but you took it out on us." Gregory was always in trouble--he had a fight every day.

"You know, Mrs. Byrd, that's the way I am every day," he went on. "I can see, but I can't read. I yell at a lot of people. I push them away, and sometimes I just hit them. In nearly every class, the teachers hand me something and say, 'Read this, and answer the questions at the end,' but I can't read. That's the way you felt when you couldn't see," he said. "You just couldn't cut it, and you got mad and took it out on us."

Another time, I assigned some homework, and Celerino said, "Mrs. Byrd, you're assigning me homework like I got a room to myself and a set of encyclopedias. Take me home this afternoon," he said. "You are going to get a different view of what it's like at my house."

I took him home. He lived in a three-room house with eight other people...wall to wall people. He said, "If

I need more help, you come to school early and I'll meet you, or you stay late and I'll stay, too; but don't give me work to do at home...there's no place to do it." He was so right.

I had Tony. And I found that I could say, "Tony, Tony, Tony ... don't talk, don't do this, don't do that," and he just kept on talking. I could walk up, put my hand on his shoulder and say, "Tony, don't talk," and that was the end of it.

I asked him, "Tony, what is all this junk? I say 'Tony this and Tony that' and you ignore me. Then I walk up to you and put my hand on your shoulder and you stop."

Tony said, "Mrs. Byrd, there are three Tony's in my family. We live in three rooms. If I stopped every time somebody said 'Tony,' I'd just stop all the time. If they want me, they grab hold of me." That made sense.

These kids can teach us so much!

BIG KIDS ARE NOT ALL THAT BIG

For those of you who teach big kids, let me remind you--they're not all that big. They still have the same need

150

to be loved and the same need to be accepted. And what you think as a teacher is still important to them, although they'll hide it every way they can.

I had a kid tell me one time when he was failing Trig, "Mrs. Byrd, I'm failing trig, and why doesn't she [his teacher] like me?"

"Billy," I said, "you're probably failing trig because you're not doing your homework, and what you need to do is get you a nice quiet place to study every day and you study in the same place at the same time ...."

"Why doesn't she like me?" he continued to ask.

"Billy, I don't think you've heard what I've said. The reason that your failing trig is...." I went through this three times and each time he'd still ask,

"But why doesn't she like me?"

Finally, exasperated, I asked, "Billy, what is more important, that you pass Trig or that you find out why she doesn't like you?"

"To find out why she doesn't like me," he responded. "I think if I knew that, I could pass Trig."

Mark was a big kid who during all four years that he was in high school, came in every morning that I was there and hugged my neck and said, "I just do this, Mrs. Byrd, 'cause you smell so good." (You don't know what that does for an old girl from Cross Plains who used to always smell like Vick's Vapor Rub all winter.) But what he knew that I knew was that his parents were never there and that he lived with a housekeeper who slept late and went to bed early and didn't speak English. He wanted somebody to know that he was alive and somebody to care--and I did.

Remember this about your kids, and don't kid yourself that what you think isn't important to them.

QUICK, FAST THINGS FOR TEACHERS TO REMEMBER

Regardless of where you teach, I want to give you some quick, easy things to remember:

* You need to reach each kid each day. I don't mean anything dramatic -- but it doesn't take much time to stand in the door and smile and pat.

* You need to create an atmosphere that says that learning is fun; learning is exciting; come on in and join the show! Say, "Curiosity is welcome!" Little kids are always curious, but we "sophisticate" it out

of kids by the time they're in the seventh grade. We need to remember that curiosity is just intelligence having a good time.

* Teach them to cope with change.

* Teach them to negotiate.

* If you don't teach them anything else, teach them to be kind. If we educate their heads and not their hearts, we're going to turn out a bunch of intellectual barbarians.

* As with parents, you don't always have to be right. It's o.k. to say, "I don't know" every once in a while.

* Teach them that most of all, we're human "beings," before we're human "doings." Feelings don't have any race, color, age, or test scores ... and still, they are the most important things about us and the things on which 90% of our decisions are made. Contrary to popular belief, I do not think the challenge of the nineties--or even the 21st Century--is who wins the technology race or who wins the information race or even who wins the math-science race. It's going to be who wins the human race.

* Last, but not least, let them know you care!

WHAT GOES AROUND, COMES AROUND-- AND TEACHERS SET THE STAGE

A lot of teachers worry about the new trends in education, such as "inclusion." I don't worry about inclusion -- maybe because I'm retired and know I'm not going to have to deal with it. But, really, when I started teaching all we had was "inclusion." There was no "gifted and talented" class--we just, after a while, grouped everybody "according to ability." There were no alternative schools or special education classes. In education, what goes around, comes around, but I believe--regardless of the trends or the kinds of schools--it is the teacher who sets the stage for our kids.

Speaking of alternative schools, I was thinking the other day that we didn't have alternative schools when I was teaching--then I realized, I was the alternative school. I had four or five preparations and had every mean kid in school that nobody else wanted -- sometimes for four or five periods a day.

Recently I was speaking to a small school district way out in West Texas, and they wanted me to visit the alternative school before I spoke to the main campus. Well, they had sixteen kids in the alternative school--fifteen of the thuggiest looking boys you ever saw, and one girl who could have matched any of them. I just had about ten minutes to spend with them. I walked in, and here they were, draped over their chairs with looks that said, "O.K. just motivate me, Old Lady, if you think you've got it in you."

"I was the alternative school when I taught," I told them. "I taught kids like you four or five periods a day."

One of the boys raised up and said, "Are you kidding? You had kids like us... and her, four or five periods a day, and you're still with us? You must have been a tough old coot."

"I was," I said, "and I may have been kind of a crazy old coot, because I liked you."

"Another thing that used to make me fighting mad," I told them, "was when I heard people say, 'those kids are stupid'. You are not stupid. How could you think up all this mean stuff you do if you were stupid?"

But, I think the one thing along with these alternative schools that we need is this: WE'VE GOT TO BELIEVE THEY CAN DO BETTER!

I've been visiting prison schools in Texas, which has been real interesting for me. In Texas, inmates used to be required and now are encouraged to go to school until they pass the GED or until they can read on the 6th grade level, unless they have some kind of handicap that keeps them from doing that. In these schools, academic classrooms are the only rooms in the buildings that are air-conditioned and they are the only places these inmates can go three hours a day and not have to do hard labor and yet, they won't go. The younger the inmates, the harder time they have getting them to go.

The prison teachers were really devoted to the cause, which was a new idea for me. I had thought the teacher turnover must be terrible, but the average time the teachers had been there was ten years. They were really committed to the idea that if we are ever going to have fewer people in prison, it is going to be through education and a change of attitude. According to the teachers, when they tried to talk to the young inmates, they'd say, "Don't talk to us. Teachers hate us; they always have. And, besides that, they think we're stupid. Don't talk to us and act like you like us."

The prison teachers told me, "If we can get them in our classes for six weeks, we've got them for however long they're here." And they had a lot of younger prisoners getting associate degrees from a local junior college. "But," they said, "we work like dogs getting a relationship built up." They told me because the inmates are so distrustful, they usually bond with one teacher, so the teachers try to conduct an almost contained classroom rather than being so departmental. It was a real eye-opener to me.

I also heard a panel discussion where troubled kids in alternative schools talked about methods used to teach them. Some of these methods seemed so dull that they would have bored the horns off of a billy goat. When they finished, the moderator (who was a kid) explained that the method of teaching that was used was not that important--it was just that it was the first time in a long time for these troubled kids that a teacher believed in them and thought they had some smarts!

When I first began teaching, we didn't have special education either. I can remember one time I had forty-nine kids in my 3rd period class. The principal brought in this little boy and said, " Mrs. Byrd, this is a new student who is going to be in your class. His name is Arlin."

"Fine," I said. That made fifty in the class.

The principal took me aside and whispered, "By the way, Mrs. Byrd, Arlin is brain-damaged."

So, I did what any self-respecting teacher would do.

I put my arm around the kid and said, "Come on in, Arlin Darlin'. We are just glad to have you in here. I want you to sit back there behind Sharon Waron and in front of Billy Nilly (thinking in rhymes). They are just the neatest kids! And this is the neatest class! And I can tell just by looking at you that you are going to fit in fine! Arlin Darlin', say hello to the class."

"Hello," Arlin said.

Then I said, "Class, say hello to Arlin Darlin', we're just going to love him!"

They said, "Hello, Arlin Darlin'."

I often thought that, without really knowing what I was doing, I had set up a good spot for this kid. The kids in that class learned to love that kid. How could you not love somebody called Arlin Darlin'? I've thought ever since then that what we, as teachers, set up for a kid is a whole lot of what determines the reaction the student gets from the other kids--or the teachers in the lounge. WE DO MAKE A DIFFERENCE IN THEIR LIVES.

THE HARDEST THING ABOUT BEING A COUNSELOR

Do you know the hardest thing about being a counselor? You always have to be pleasant. You know, it didn't make any difference if I were suffering from hot flashes and hemorrhoids at the same time, when that door opened, I had to be pleasant. Whoever's coming in has problems of his own; he doesn't want to listen to mine. It was much easier when I was teaching. I used to tell my kids the first day that I had them, "Kids, if you have it with your parents at home before you come to first period class, come tell me. Say, 'Mrs. Byrd, I had a terrible morning before I got here. Give me a little time to sit back and get my act together.' I understand that. If you've had it with your third-period teacher, don't come to my class the fourth period and make me mad. Instead, come in and say, 'I had it with Miss Pitt third period. Please give me a little time to get it together.' Don't pull this on me three times a week, but when it really happens, if you'll tell me, I can understand."

I'm convinced that most discipline problems we have--especially at the first of the period--have nothing to do with us. They are garbage that has been collected from somewhere else during the day.

By the same token, I told the kids, "If I've had it with the Big Byrd before I get to school in the morning, I'm going to tell you and you act accordingly." Sometimes, I would come in and say, "All right, kids, I've had it with him this morning before I left home. If you are going to breathe, do it quietly." The interesting thing is, you just had to tell your first period class--the rest of them would tippy-toe in.

But, as a counselor, I didn't have that privilege. I had to be pleasant.

THE LOST SHEEP SYNDROME

If there's one thing we, as counselors and teachers, have brought to our work from the Bible, it's the lost-sheep syndrome. We can be doing wonderful things with 98% of the kids we work with, but we spend all our time worrying about the two we can't help. That's what we talk about in the lounge; that's what we talk about when we get home; that's what we talk about all the time.

Now, I'm a great believer in not missing anyone if we can help it. But, let's give ourselves credit for some of the good things we do and quit spending all this energy thinking about, and worrying about, and talking only about the two that we missed.

Dr. Embree, my mentor in counseling once said to me, "Toody, you want to hit a home run every time you get up to bat. Even the pros don't do that. You're lucky to get a base hit every once in a while. They strike out a lot more often than they hit home runs. And, face it, Toody, some days the game is just rained out!"

Take anything for success.

We really need to remember this.

OUR DRUG REHAB PROGRAM

This is, of course, an unbiased opinion, but under the watchful eye of Kappie Bliss, we had one of the State's best drug abuse programs at our school. It wasn't a program that we found and then said, now we've got to find some kids to stick in it. What we saw were these kids who were real smart, but they weren't doing anything in their classes; they were having the same kinds of behavior problems. We counselors didn't know what was the matter, but we knew that something was. So, we finally got them together and found that they all lived with at least one alcoholic parent or sibling. As counselors, we had all read enough or gone to enough workshops to know the cycles that go on in alcoholic families.

We made a proposal to our school board that we would run a drug abuse program. The kids referred themselves. Teachers could refer them, but usually it was the kids themselves. We also had drug dogs that came on campus. I want you to understand that before they came I told the administrators, "You'll bring those drug dogs on the campus over my dead body!" We had drug dogs. But I'll tell you why I bought into that. We had freshmen who would stay in my office during lunch because they were afraid to go out because somebody always tried to sell them drugs, or give them to them, or force them on them. And I thought, "No kid at my school is going to be afraid to go out at noon." So we had these drug dogs.

If a kid were picked up with drugs, he was suspended from school for six days, but the parent could appeal immediately, and he'd go into our program. We had very few parents who did not appeal. Sometimes, the kid would be picked up because there was marijuana in his car. I had one father who came to school livid! "My son deserves an apology!" he said, "That was my paraphernalia. Somebody needs to apologize to my son!"

"I'm with you," I said. "This is a good kid. Somebody does need to apologize--why don't you?"

I want you to understand I was not his favorite person.

Originally we thought we might have five groups running--we ended up with twenty groups with eight kids in each group meeting once a week. We had four more groups with eight kids in each group who had already been through drug rehab-programs--and we could have run twice that many. We had groups that met at night for the parents of these kids, and do you know who got them there? The kids did! Every teacher in our high school was trained, so we had meetings where we would involve everybody--kids, counselors, teachers, and parents. There was not any of this, "Don't take this kid out of my class for group."

This program was a wonderful thing that we just did by the seat of our pants. We just saw a need and did something to help.

FOR "AT-RISK" KIDS, THE SOLUTION BEGINS WITH THE HEART

We now talk a lot about involving parents and the community--that we are all in this together. For years, schools have given lip service about wanting parents to be part of the team, but we didn't teach them the plays and didn't really even want them in the huddle. Now, we don't have any choice. In lots of states, it's mandated that schools have to get parents involved.

But, while prisons will show that over 90% of prison inmates are school dropouts, all dropouts don't go to prison--a lot of them stay right where they are, marry another school dropout, and have five kids who won't go to school. So, do you know what we do when we begin to design programs to keep kids in school? We form a committee. On the committee we put the principal, some teachers, maybe a counselor, and--if we really want to impress somebody--we get a PhD from the college or from the State Department of Education (the kind who pops in and pops off and pops out). We get these people who've never done anything but go to school--and they're going to design a program to keep kids who don't want to be there in the first place in school? These kids are coming from families where their parents dropped out of school. It appears to me that we need to get to the parents and ask, "Why'd you drop out? Why do you send your kids to school? What would make it a good place for your kids to be?"

I bet I've been on fifteen attendance committees at school, and instead of trying to figure out why the kids didn't come to school, we just tried to devise better methods to punish them because they didn't get there. We put

the same people on the committee as we did on the drop-
out committees. Sometimes we put a parent on the committee...the one who had a master's degree from Southern
Methodist University, had children in the gifted and talented program, and stayed at home and watched the papers to
see when the sales were going to be on at Neiman Marcus.
I used to ask, "Why don't we ever put any kids on these
committees?" Well, the principal put three kids on the
committee--do you know which three: the three kids with
perfect attendance. They didn't know why kids didn't
come to school--they hadn't missed a day in years. And
besides that, they were the meanest members of the com-
mittee--they wanted to "sock it to them."

In my school district, the only thing we ever found to
work with truancy and drop-outs was to group the "at-
risk" students with a teacher who cared about them, and
have that teacher call them or go out to their house if they
didn't have a telephone, and say, "I missed you. It's not
the same when you're not here."

That made a difference, and it didn't cost very much
... just a little time and a lot of caring. But I have to give
you a warning. You cannot begin this way and let up.
Those kids are so conscious of not fitting in and of people
not caring for them, that if you miss one little thing, it

confuses them. I used to sell doughnuts every morning in the cafeteria for the Student Council, and every morning, Rudy, one of the kids in my drop-out program would come in, put his arm around me, pat me, and say, "Hello, Mrs. Byrd, I want a doughnut."

Every morning, I'd put my arm around Rudy, pat him, wink, and say, "O.K. Rudy, we'll get you a dough-nut."

One day, during last period, Rudy knocked on my door and asked, "Mrs. Byrd, what are you mad at me for?"

"Rudy, I'm not mad at you," I said. "I saw you this morning; I hugged you; I sold you a doughnut. What's the matter?"

"You didn't wink," he said. "I worried about it all day."

These kids needed to know we cared. The drop-out program worked. The kids came to school! They didn't have any more money than they'd had before; they didn't have any more parental push than they'd had before, but they did have a safe place to come and someone to love them once they got there, and someone who missed them when they weren't there. That was the cheapest drop-out program in the State of Texas, and it worked so well that they did away with it.

I think maybe we ought to also ask some of these people who are having the problems for some ideas. However, parents who were school dropouts don't want to come to school to talk to us--school doesn't have happy memories for them. So, if they won't come in, we have to face it--we are going to have to go out. But, in general, I believe most parents want their kids to learn and that they want them to come to school. I also think they want their kids to be involved, and that they want to be involved, too. But, they are just real hesitant and appre-hensive. I believe we have to make school a good place for both these kids and their parents.

When we talk about "at-risk" kids and kids on drugs, I don't think that the solutions begin with the curriculum; I think they begin with the heart. We've got to truly want to help them. We have to instill in them the belief that we want to help them enough that they'll trust us enough to want to do something better. And we need to get them young enough, so we can prevent some of the problems.

Someday I'm going to do a book with nothing but pictures from the permanent records. You look at those kids and see that for the first two years, those are the hap-piest kids in the world. Then they lose their two front teeth, and they are still pretty happy. But watch the pictures and you can see where we lost them.

We get so hung up about the drug problem in the upper grades of the middle school and high school, which is only the manifestation of the problem. I know this man who goes around the country saying he can spot kids in the third grade who are probably going to have drug problems, but instead of helping them, we start punishing them. I truly believe that these kids don't have to have a lot of people believe in them--but they have to have one!

For those of you who are teachers who care, I believe that every year there is one kid who would not make it without you. I think the wonderful thing about that is that we don't know for sure which one it is. I am still getting calls and letters from kids who graduated from Westlake High School fifteen or twenty years ago, calling to tell me where they are and what they are doing. A former student called me the other day from Chicago and said, "Mrs. Byrd, I've got my PhD, and I'm going to be the head of the department at a new college, and I was trying to get up my nerve to go for the first day tomorrow. I did what I do every time I need to buckle down and get my courage up. I read this thing I wrote in my diary that you said to me when I was a junior in high school." This kid had more problems than almost any kid I'd had. She was in the drug scene, and she had terrible family problems.

"Mrs. Byrd," she continued, "you may not even remember this, but I came in hysterical that day and took your letter opener and started hacking up your bulletin board and was screaming and crying." (I remembered it!)

"I can remember saying to you, 'Mrs. Byrd, I am so screwed up. I am so into the drug scene. I think I'm schizophrenic, and I am always going to be a mess!'

"Do you know what you did?" she asked me. "You came around from behind your desk, and you put your arms around me and said, 'Do you know what I think, Mary? I think you're kind of wonderful. I know this is a hard time, but I think you're always going to be kind of wonderful!'"

"I just let out this bloodcurdling scream, ran out the door, ran home (I can still see you standing there with your mouth open), and I wrote in my diary exactly what you said before I forgot it."

"It's taken me a long time to get where I've gotten, but this page of my diary looks like it has been passed on for fifteen generations. I thought you maybe needed to know about this, Mrs. Byrd."

I did need to know about it.

And I'm not telling you this to "tooteth my own horn" (although I do think that's important). I'm telling you because I think this kind of thing happens to every one of you who works with kids. You just may not know it for fifteen years--or you may never know it, but it does. Don't ever forget how important you are.

TOODY BYRD TALKS ABOUT LIFE

BEING RETIRED

Being retired is a wonderful place to find yourself. It is kind of like being a grandmother or the past president of an organization. It's where you've already messed up everybody as much as you can, and now you can sit back and tell everyone else how to do it right. You won't be judged by it, and you can become an authority. I used to think I would become an expert until my friend, Mary Adele, said an "ex" is a has-been, and a "spurt" is a drip under pressure, so I decided I would be a consultant. But I changed my mind about this, since consultants are usually brought in from out of state, and just pop in, pop off, and pop out! So I have finally decided to become an authority. My dad always used to say, "Toody, you need to make your life good for something--even if it's just as a horrible example."

Just as soon as I get out of the city limits of Austin, I am an authority.   Now my prayer every night is one my friend, Nancy, taught me: "Use me in thy works, Oh Lord...if only in an advisory capacity."

THINGS I'VE LEARNED IN WHAT BERT JONES CALLS THE "TWILIGHT OF A MEDIOCRE CAREER"

Let me give you some quick thoughts I have learned or stolen from various or sundry people or places over my life:

* The first one I got from Abraham Lincoln (I didn't get it from him personally). But both Lincoln and I have learned we are about as happy as we make up our minds to be.

* I've learned that happiness is not the destination, it's the trip. I'm always hearing somebody come in and say, "Just as soon as we get all three kids through college, we're going to take time to travel and be happy." Or, "Just as soon as we get both cars and the house paid for, we're going to spend some time doing things together and be happy." Listen, you're not going to be happy--you're going to be old!

* I've learned that I usually see what I look for.

* I've learned that of all the labor-saving devices....

money is the best one.

* I've learned that if I want to win the lottery, I've got to buy a ticket.

* I've learned that success is never final, and failure is never fatal.

* I've learned that when it hits the fan, it will not come back equally distributed.

* I've learned that the loudest "Boo's" usually come from the people in the free seats.

* I've learned that friends may come and friends may go, but enemies accumulate.

* I have finally learned to cooperate--that 'tis better to struggle with a sick jackass than to carry the wood myself.

* I've learned that life is the most exciting thing in the world that's ever happened to me and I'm glad I didn't miss it! A kid asked me just before graduation, "Mrs. Byrd, what would you say if somebody told you that you had six days to live?"
I said, "I'd say, Wonderful, because that's six more days than I know I have today." And I said, "I'll tell you something else, Kid, if I knew for sure I just had

six days, I sure would put off a bunch of stuff."

* I've learned to accentuate the positive and eliminate the negative.

* I've even learned not to mess with Mister In-Between. I've learned to take one side or the other--the only thing you find consistently in the middle of the road are yellow stripes and dead armadillos.

* The greatest thing I've learned is to love uncondi-tionally. Now don't get me wrong, I haven't learned to love everybody. But the people I love, I love unconditionally. There are no more, "I'll love you ifs" or "I love you buts" or "If you loved me, you'ds". I said to my kids and I hope they say to theirs, "I love you. It's a gift; take it. You don't have to earn it with good looks, or good grades, or even good behavior. It's a gift I give to you because I'm your mama! Nothing you ever do or say is going to make me love you any less or any more. That does not mean I'm going to like everything you do. That does not mean I'm not going to set some boundaries and stick to them. It does not mean I'm not going to

ride your sore back sometimes. It does not even mean I may not shake you while I hug you, but I love you. You don't ever have to worry about losing that." And you know, the other end of unconditional love is if they love you back, it's a fringe benefit, but there's no string attached. It's made my life a whole lot simpler. It's a gift I've given myself.

* Life is like a bluebird, Omar the poet has said; some years he sits in your window and sings and some years he dumps on your head. You just have to hope the singing years outnumber the dumping years.

* I don't know if Robert Browning knew what he was talking about when he said, "Grow old along with me, the best is yet to be."....but it's the best offer I've had lately, and I'm going to take him up on it. I hope you'll join me, and may we all live as long as we're useful, and laugh...and learn...and love as long as we live.

T. BYRD ROADRUNNER PRESS
107 Tallstar Drive • Austin, Texas 78734

Please send me _____ copies of *Toody Byrd Talks...* @ $14.50 each (incl. tax &

postage), or *please send a gift copy of *Toody Byrd Talks...* from

_____ @ $14.50 each to:

Name _____

Address_____

City _____ State _____ Zip_____

Make checks payable to T. Byrd Roadrunner Press
A gift card with your name will be included with the book.

T. BYRD ROADRUNNER PRESS
107 Tallstar Drive • Austin, Texas 78734

Please send me _____ copies of *Toody Byrd Talks...* @ $14.50 each (incl. tax &

postage), or *please send a gift copy of *Toody Byrd Talks...* from

_____ @ $14.50 each to:

Name _____

Address_____

City _____ State _____ Zip_____

Make checks payable to T. Byrd Roadrunner Press
A gift card with your name will be included with the book.

T. BYRD ROADRUNNER PRESS
107 Tallstar Drive • Austin, Texas 78734

Please send me _____ copies of *Toody Byrd Talks...* @ $14.50 each (incl. tax &

postage), or *please send a gift copy of *Toody Byrd Talks...* from

_____ @ $14.50 each to:

Name _____

Address_____

City _____ State _____ Zip_____

Make checks payable to T. Byrd Roadrunner Press
A gift card with your name will be included with the book.

Notes

Notes